RICHES
R*to*AGS

WYNONA ROGERS

One Woman's Story of Betrayal
and Redemption

RICHES
R*to*AGS

Keep it light
God Bless
Pearl

TATE PUBLISHING
AND **ENTERPRISES**, LLC

Published by Tate Publishing & Enterprises, LLC
127 E. Trade Center Terrace | Mustang, Oklahoma 73064 USA
1.888.361.9473 | www.tatepublishing.com

Tate Publishing is committed to excellence in the publishing industry. The company reflects the philosophy established by the founders, based on Psalm 68:11,
"The Lord gave the word and great was the company of those who published it."

Book design copyright © 2013 by Tate Publishing, LLC. All rights reserved.
Cover design by Rodrigo Adolfo
Interior design by Joana Quilantang

Published in the United States of America

ISBN: 978-1-62510-844-9
1. Biography & Autobiography / General
2. Biography & Autobiography / Personal Memoirs
13.08.01

DEDICATION

To God for his comfort and for his blessings in my past and the ones he continues to give me daily.

David T. Rogers Sr., my Super Dave and father, my inspiration and hero.

Margaret E Rogers, my mom, for all the love and support she has given me throughout my life.

David J. Schoen, my son and Little Dude, for the strength he gave me in our troubled times.

David L. Salter, my husband, for all the love and support he has selflessly given me and continues to do so every day.

ACKNOWLEDGMENTS

David L. Salter

SPECIAL THANKS

Margaret E. Rogers
Nancy Norris
David J. Schoen
David L. Salter
Wade Burleson
US Secret Service
Gulf Shores Police Department
Pastor Rick Long

TABLE OF CONTENTS

Note from the Author

My name is Wynona Rogers. What you are about to read really happened to me. After you read it, you may think I made it up. I can assure you: it's all real. Even the guys in Hollywood would have had a time making up what happened to me. It is mainly about the years I owned Starfish Insurance in Gulf Shores, Alabama, and how a few crooked people can decimate people's lives. More importantly, I hope with God's love and grace, we can carry on. May what happened to me never happen to you. May you receive the miracles you need to see you through. I'm a redneck at heart and love to see people smile so I've thrown in a little redneck humor to boot. When life's train wrecks find you, know that the best humor always comes from the deepest pain. Roll with the punches and never stop laughing and smiling. One of my clients gave me some good advice: don't sweat the small stuff—and it is all small.

I am not only proud of publishing my tale but I am enormously proud of Little Dude, my awesome son.

The artwork in the book is his. Since he was three (when he was introduced to paper instead of my nice white walls), he has shown enormous amounts of talent in art. Now that he is older, he's been developing his skills on the basketball court. Who knows, maybe he will follow my dad's footsteps and play college ball at Auburn.

God bless and enjoy.

PREFACE

Riches to Rags: One Woman's Story of Betrayal and Redemption is about how God will carry you through anything. If you see only one set of footprints in the sand, they are not yours. It is the good Lord above carrying you. During my troubles, I sometimes gave up on God. God never gave up on me. Instead he was there comforting me and showing me his love. My story is also a mystery. The book has a twist at the end that I didn't even see coming. The parts you don't enjoy, blame my husband. Wink. May God's angels always protect you.

In the Beginning

I was only two years old when I decided to sell insurance for a living. My daddy, Super Dave, was a district manager at the time with a major insurance firm. His gift of gab and genuine desire to help people made him a good living for his family. People called him a gentle giant. At six foot four and a half, he could be intimidating, but you could never meet a sweeter man. He never raised his voice or had a bad word to say about anybody, including the ones who stole from him. He retired from his role as a district manager at age sixty-five but was called back to work as an agent for another fourteen years.

Before me, my two sisters, and Mom, Super Dave graduated from Auburn University; he landed a job in Foley, Alabama, as an agriculture teacher. He had grown up farming and being the preacher's son. During WWII he was enlisted in a reserve group that ultimately made it to Europe. They deployed him and about two hundred soldiers into the worst places in Hitler's Germany. During the time they were there, they found shelter in an old castle where they would play poker with the spoils of war they found laying around, some of which he brought back to the states when he returned. Since Super Dave was the commanding officer, he got dibs on sleeping arrangements. It was the king's suite; it was for him. The next day he woke up and went downstairs. He was surprised to see his whole platoon drunk. His soldiers had found the wine cellar while he was sawing logs. When I asked him what he did, he said, "There was but one thing to do, and I did it—drink." My dad might drink one beer a year so I always wondered just how many years' worth he had that day.

When the concentration camp at Dachau was liberated, my father and others secured the area. The scenes he must have endured, I can only imagine. He never talked about it except when he told us how he got a Nazi SS officer's sword as a reminder of the tragedy. General Patton kept Daddy around even when he was ready to head back to the states. Before he made his way out of Germany, one of his main tasks was to use his knowledge and education of farming to help the German people recover from the carnage.

When Daddy returned home to the States, he found his teaching job had been filled. He was in a pickle like a lot of other soldiers who had been replaced at their jobs. That's about the time when the phone rang. It was his old college buddy EJ. EJ had founded what would become one of the major insurance companies in Alabama and offered Super Dave a job. Without much else going for him, he gladly accepted his friend's offer. EJ hired him as the district manager. He handled from Montgomery, Alabama, to the sugar-white sands of

Gulf Shores. He loved his job. One day a man applied for a position as an agent. He had a job in a radio station but didn't make enough to provide for his wife and five kids. Daddy hired him on the spot. Years later, Brother Bill would become the company's vice president.

It was a rule with ALFA Insurance Company to retire district managers at age sixty-five. They retired Daddy and hired him back that same day to be an agent. Daddy had always wanted to go back to Foley, Alabama. They had an opening there so they transferred him. Daddy worked as an agent in Foley until he was seventy-nine years old. Again the company told him it was time to retire so, reluctantly, he did.

Mom and Super Dave started buying beach property in the sixties. Daddy's sisters always ribbed him about buying land he couldn't plant tomatoes on. What it did have on it, though, was four cottages. They rented them to snow birds in the winter and mostly weekenders in the summer months. Nineteen seventy-nine was the year Hurricane Fredrick hit Gulf Shores, Alabama. There was about a quarter of one of the cottages left and not a trace of the others when they let us inspect them. When the time came to rebuild, six nice duplex condos sat in their place. Around 2001, we finally sold the beach property for four million dollars. Mom, Baby Doll (my younger sister), Chickee (my older sister), and I all got a cool million. After the IRS got a forth of mine, I was still sitting pretty on seven hundred and fifty thousand dollars. Two years later, adjacent property was going for forty million. At my request part of our negotiations did include a penthouse in the new building when it was built. Not bad for some dirt you couldn't grow anything in!

I grew up in Foley and graduated high school there. After high school I went to Faulkner Junior College in Bay Minett, Alabama. After two years, I transferred to Auburn University. That same year my younger sister, Baby Doll, started her first year at Auburn. She rented a small apartment across town with two of her friends. After they got settled in, Baby Doll decided to refresh with a shower.

"Where's the hamster?" she asked as she exited the bathroom.

"You know we aren't allowed pets. You better not have brought one in here," Pricilla scolded back.

"I'm talking about where you put dirty clothes, you idiot, not a pet," Baby Doll replied.

Both of the roommates fell down on the floor in seizures from laughing so hard.

"It's not a hamster, you country hick. It's a *hamper*," said the other roommate between hyperventilating and laughing.

"I'm gonna choke Wynona for teaching me that one," came the response from a now teeth-gritting Baby Doll.

It was meant as a harmless ribbing. I hope Baby Doll didn't wait too long to forgive me. You can trust people. Sometimes you just need to verify. Advice I wish I had taken more myself.

The year I left Auburn, Daddy had won a trip to Disney World. Daddy, Mom, and I loaded up in the family car to cruise to Orlando. The first night there we met for a casual company dinner. We sat at a table with Bubba (the company VP) and his wife, Madison. As we waited for our food order to be taken, Daddy explained to Bubba that I wanted a job selling insurance. Bubba just looked at me over the top of his menu and said, "I am ready when you are."

"I'm ready right now," I said.

"Okay then! When I get back, I'll call the local district manager then give you a call."

To this day they have a rule that they will not hire anyone under twenty-five years old. I was only twenty-three. The next Monday I was in a near panic as I waited for some news. Finally, Daddy called and let me know he had heard from Bubba. He told me I needed to be there by nine o'clock the next day. Interview day came, and I put on my office clothes and a huge smile and made a mad dash to my destiny. The district manager, Doug, hired me on the spot. They had no place to put me so they opened an office in Gulf Shores, Alabama. My first month's commission check was nothing but zeros. I thought it was a hoot. I wanted to frame it and hang it on my office wall.

I worked for ALFA Insurance Company for twenty-six years, which is nearly unheard of. Most newbie agents last less than two years. When they hired me, I was determined not to disappoint my daddy. At first I had to cold-call clients (pick people from the phone book), which I hated. I started by calling people at home. After I got the 356 hang-ups, I realized this was a bad idea. I decided one day to cold call businesses at work. That worked much better. That's how my client list really started growing. Five years in and I was pulling down six figures in commissions. At twenty years I regularly broke the $200K mark.

Three marriages came and went. With the third came the best gift I have ever received: my son. Little Dude, as I call him, and I were always together doing cool stuff. When he was young, he had asthma. The doctors recommended swimming to help with his breathing. At the time we lived in Foley. In the winter for a few years, just like a couple of snow birds, we rented a condo that had an indoor pool so he could swim year round. How we longed to live on the island full time.

In 2002 my friend and realtor Melody took me to the most awesome property. The huge lot had these live oaks that were covered with Spanish moss. It sat high on a twenty-foot-tall bluff overlooking the quiet side of Perdido Bay. I fell in love with it and had her give me the bottom line. I wrote her a check for it on the spot. By May of 2004, I managed to get what I had hoped would be my retirement house built. The house wasn't huge by today's standard, only about fourteen hundred square feet with super-wide wrap-around porches. And of course, it was painted my favorite color—purple. The lot was big enough that I planned one day to build a house for my son, too. Little Dude and I had it made literally in the shade. Thanks to the blessings of a great job and good investments by Mom and Daddy, we had no bills, a new house, and reason for jubilation.

I sold a piece of vacant property I owned and with money to burn, decided to take Little Dude to Disney World to celebrate. At age four he couldn't ride all the rides so we had a ball on the ones we could. One day as we left to go to the park, he scooted past me and came to a stop at our hotel room door.

"Stop!" he commanded me. As I did what he requested, he bowed and gestured with his arm, "Ladies first."

I was so proud of him! I taught him well, and I was pleased. Fishing for a compliment, I asked, "That is so sweet. Who did you learn that from?"

"Scooby-Doo."

I was crushed, but I couldn't help but bust out laughing.

Little Dude spent his time playing, swimming, and painting. At seven years old, he was the youngest artist to have a booth at the world famous Gulf Shores Shrimp Festival. His skill had improved since his red-crayon sketches on the living room walls. He got the attention of a reporter who just had to do a story on him. Little Dude would be the first in our family to make the front page of a newspaper, but not the only one.

Two and a half decades of relative calm and prosperity in my life gave out when Hurricane Ivan came to Orange Beach.

Ivan the Terrible Comes to Town

Hurricane Ivan laid waste to the Alabama and Florida Gulf Coast on September 15, 2004. There was plenty of devastation that Ivan left behind. There were whole houses missing from the beach, high-rise buildings flat on the ground, and not a structure anywhere without heavy damage. The tidal surge came in two miles into the city. It was not the devastation that got to me but the horror stories of people who stayed. You do not have to be on the beach to have a hurricane party. The news will show you plenty of photos of before, during, and after a hurricane. Little Dude and I had left since we lived in the purple house on the bay. Law enforcement and the National Guard would not let anyone back on the island for two weeks. Most of the roads were impassable. The worst thing was that they had to let the Gulf of Mexico rescind back to the beach so they could look for dead bodies.

When they let us go back to our house, I just knew there would be nothing there. To my surprise, nothing had happened to it. There were trees down in the yard and trash on our private beach. The ceiling fans on the porch did not make it. But that was about all. The next day I went back to the office and back to work. The office was open from 6:00 a.m. to 6:00 p.m. The whole time the phones never stopped, and people never stopped coming in to file their claims. I thought that was a nightmare. Weeks flew by without a break.

When I first started taking claims, I would listen to everything anyone had to say. The people I thought would be mean were nice. The people I thought would be nice were mean. Go figure. So many had lost so much. One friend of mine from school lived a block from the lagoon. She knew her house would flood but never thought about how high. She and her husband put all their wedding photos and their son's baby picture on their bed. They thought it would be safe. Hurricane Ivan was forty-two feet tall when he hit the beach. She lived about a mile from it. Her whole house went under water. Everything was ruined. She was upset and started yelling at me like I had ordered the hurricane. I finally had to ask her to leave and to come back when she had cooled off.

I had clients living in their cars because their houses had been destroyed. They had no money and no place to go. They just parked their car in their driveway, waiting on the adjuster to come by and pay their claim. I had one family living in a bedroom because that was the only part of the house that had a roof.

I had worked fifteen days straight for twelve hours a day. It was heart-wrenching to hear all the horror stories of people who stayed and did not make it. Most deaths never made the news. One man who came in to file a claim told me his son was a paramedic in Perdido Key Florida. While I pulled up his information, he told me that when his son had bagged his sixtieth body, he quit. On his last day, his son saw a child's doll on the beach. When he leaned over to pick it up, he discovered the body of a three-year-old girl still holding onto it. After that one I had to go outside and get some fresh air. All I could think was how glad I was that I had taken Little Dude somewhere safe.

People need to know when government authorities make mandatory evacuations, do not question why. Just do it. They are trying to save your life.

A man came in to file a claim on his beach house. While sitting in front of my desk, he told me about his neighbor. His neighbor's son was going to college in Mississippi. When he learned there was a hurricane coming, he and seventeen of his friends came to Gulf Shores. They had never had a hurricane party and wanted to see the hurricane up close. After the hurricane, the police, army reserve, and federal agents went door to door to see if they could find any survivors. When they went to his neighbor's house, they found nine dead bodies. They never found the other nine.

Another client lived on the south side of the lagoon where there was a tremendous amount of debris. The city had cleared the road off and pushed everything to the side. After a few days, he started smelling something awful and called FEMA. FEMA said they would send someone down to check it out. They found nothing when they looked. It was only when the city started picking up the debris on the side of the road that they discovered a dead man and woman. No one knew them or where they had come from. To this day dozens of the victims of Ivan remain unidentified and unclaimed.

I was about to take another claim when a man stormed into the office. He had a house half a mile from the beach. He had paid cash for his house and had elected not to buy flood insurance. The man broke the line and stopped in front of my desk and pointed his finger in my face.

"You refused to sell me flood insurance, and now I have a seventy-thousand-dollar loss," he accused.

"I don't get paid for giving quotes. You refused yourself coverage when you chose not to buy the insurance I quoted you. So don't blame me for you being too cheap to buy what I suggested you needed," I shot back, calm and matter-of-factly.

"I'm going to kick your butt," he yelled, the veins in his forehead throbbing.

He just thought he was mad. I was furious. I slammed my pen on my desk, and it bounced toward him.

"That's it, dude!" I yelled back. "If you want to try me, we can step out to the parking lot, and we can see who beats whom. I'm tired of people like you going postal on me. I didn't order the hurricane!" I said as I began to come from behind my desk.

"What are you doing?" he asked as he took a few steps back.

"I'm calling you out, dude. You want to go postal, so let's go!"

"Hold it, Wynona! I'm sorry. Can we please start over?" he said softly.

"Yes, sir. The ball's in your court."

"I would like to buy some flood insurance, if that's okay with you."

"You can buy it when you have your current repairs made and I have inspected the property," I answered.

"Thank you, Wynona, I'll be in touch then," he said as he got up with as he turned to leave.

It was lunchtime, and I needed a break from the circus of my office for a bit. Across the street was the only operational hamburger joint. All the local law enforcement and all the federal workers staged their operations there. As I walked in, I spotted a friend and walked over.

"What's up, Wynona? You look a little upset," he remarked.

"A client of mine just threatened to beat me up. Can you believe that crap?"

"Well, my money would have been on you, girl! I'll see if I can help." He chuckled.

The next day I was at work taking more claims when I was interrupted when Judge Will walked in.

"Got a pen? Write this number down. 555-2525," he instructed.

"What's the number for, Judge?" I asked.

"It's my cell number. You call me when the next SOB threatens you, princess, and I'll make sure they cool off in the crossbar motel for a while." He was serious.

As he turned around and walked out of my office, I felt relieved. Finally someone really cared. Apparently the word spread around, because I didn't have anymore trouble with irate clients.

It took almost a year of hard work and long hours to get the claims finished. I had gotten tired of people hitting me up when I was at the grocery store for their claim check. One man told me he was not leaving the store until I wrote him a check. I explained that I did not write the claims check. All I did was take the information and give it to the adjuster. He said he was still not leaving until I wrote him his check. I just shook my head and told him he would be there a very long time. I grabbed my groceries and left. When I got home, I ripped ALFA Insurance Company side signs off from the side of my H2. I figured that way I would have less problems. It worked. The phone calls kept coming at home and work, but in time that would slow down, too.

I told my clients for years if something happened, ALFA Insurance Company would take care of us. The company considered me family and loved me. Was I ever wrong. ALFA Insurance Company did not take care of them or me. I had to reopen 90 percent of the claims we took. ALFA Insurance Company had gone low on the claim payments. They owed the clients more money. I refiled everyone of them. When it was done, I was tired of ALFA Insurance Company and the way they did business. I put in my two weeks' noticed and decided to retire. My district manager said he thought it was best when I told him. I worked out my two weeks and went home to the purple house.

Had it not been for people like Mr. Tom, I'm not sure I would have survived. After Daddy passed away, Mr. Tom would stop by and drink coffee with me a couple times a week. As he explained it, "Wynona, your dad was my best friend. Now that he has gone to be with Jesus, I want to honor him and be here for you." About once a month he'd cook up the best ribs and drop them by.

Now that he too has passed on to be with Jesus, I cherish the memory of his visits and those ribs. For twenty some odd years, Mr. Ran (another of Daddy's old friends) had me keep a key to their beach house. I guarded that key with my life. Even though he would have let me stay there at anytime, I never did. Mr. Ran sent his daughter once to pick up the key and told her, "When you're done, don't give it to anyone except Wynona." It was getting to help people like Mr. Tom and Mr. Ran that made the career I had chosen worthwhile.

BUILDING MY EMPIRE

That was the best summer ever. Little Dude and I played the whole time. Fall finally came, and Little Dude had to go back to school. A month of sitting at home by myself and I was bored. I decided to start my own insurance company. I could be my own boss, go barefooted at the office, and make my own hours. What a great idea. I was really looking forward to selling insurance and helping people out on the Gulf Coast. Looking back now, I should have stayed retired and found a hobby. God had different plans for me. God put me through what he did so I could write this book and spread his love. I could blame God on what happened next, but it is not his fault. He has always been there for me. I just have not always been there for him. God is a great God. It is the devil that has tried to ruin my life. Somewhere in the Bible, there is a verse that says God will not give you more than you can take. I reckon he thought I could handle a lot.

I called my old regional manager, Dwayne. I asked him if he could give me a list of insurance companies to write for. He informed me that one of his old district

managers had quit and had started his own independent insurance company. I just needed to call him and get
that information. His name was George. I picked up
and called him at his office in Birmingham, Alabama.

We meet the next day. He explained I could sign a
contract with him. He would not be my boss; I would
be my own. He had all the companies and contact
information. All I had to do was pay his 20 percent of
my commissions. I thought that was fair and agreed.
After I signed I asked him for a copy. He explained he
only had the one I signed. When he got back to the
office, he would make me a copy and mail it to me,
which he never did. A couple of years later this would
haunt me.

I went the next day and rented an office space in
an old bank that had been converted. There was a lot
to do as far as buying office furniture and hiring a secretary. I ran into an old high school friend that day at
the phone office. She asked me what I was doing now
that I no longer worked for ALFA. I told her I had
started my own company and was looking for a secretary. She said she had a job but her sister was looking. I
gave her my cell phone number and told her to tell her
sister to call. The next day she called, and we sat up a
time that afternoon for her to come to the purple house
for the interview. Later that afternoon I was sitting on
the back porch waiting for school to get out when Tara
showed up. We sat on the porch and talked for an hour.
She said she had plenty of bookkeeping experience and
would be happy to learn the insurance business. I hired
her and told her to start the next day.

The first month I was open, I sold one car policy and made thirty dollars. I heard if you start a business, it takes three to five years for it to take off. I found that to be true. The first year was slow. It had finally started to grow, and we needed a bigger office space. I found an office right down the road in a two-story strip mall. It was on the second floor behind a busy restaurant. It was one room with a bathroom. I thought it was great and rented it. We moved, and I decided to hire a full-time bookkeeper. Tara had gotten her insurance agents license and was having a hard time keeping up. Her selling insurance had been a good idea, but letting her keep the books was not. No matter how many times I showed her which forms went with the different policies, she kept getting half of it wrong. The other half was just not done. I put an AD in the local newspaper for a full-time bookkeeper. That is when I met Barbara. Barbara saw the AD and called to make an appointment for an interview. She was busy for the next two days but could come on Friday. I told her that would be great. Anytime would work for me.

Barbara showed up Friday at nine o'clock sharp. She was dressed for success and had even dyed her hair black for the job. It was a huge contrast to me and my flip-flops. During the interview I reviewed her résumé with her.

"I see you worked for the City of Liberty in Mississippi. What were your duties there?"

"I made deposits, prepared payroll taxes, presented balance sheets directly to the mayor, and assisted with budget planning," she boasted.

"Let me check your references, but I think I'd like to have you on my team. I'll call you early next week," I told her.

After she left I immediately called the number to mayor's office she had given me.

"Hi, I'm calling in regards to Barbara. She listed you as a reference on her job application, and I was wondering if you could tell me about her work with your city," I explained.

"Oh man, do we miss her! She knew everything around here. She did most of it herself. She was really good with the bookwork. Tell her we all said hello when you see her again," the receptionist said with sincerity.

As I hung up the phone, I started to daydream about how nice it would be to finally have someone competent to take care of the mundane bookwork so I could get back to my love of selling insurance. I decided not to make her wait until Monday for my call and began dialing her number.

"Hey, Barbara, how's Monday at eight sound to you?"

"Great to me! See you then!"

For the next several months, everyone seemed to get along. One day Barbara had her son, Gregory, and his friend, Joshua, stop by. Gregory was taller than Joshua and carried himself with great confidence—almost arrogant. Joshua was more of the "shrinking-violet" type, all slumped over with his eyes fixed on the floor. They worked across the street at the furniture store.

The furniture store was having a Christmas party, and Gregory wanted his parents to come. Barbara agreed, and they left. When the door shut behind them, Barbara asked me if I would like to go. I said yes; it sounded like fun.

Before the week ended, I had decided I had had enough of Tara. I was constantly fixing her mistakes and my work had doubled. The friction in the air was unbearable. Finally, it was time to eat.

"See you in an hour," Tara grunted as she left.

"Barbara, cut Tara a check for her last week's pay. When she gets back, I'm sending her packing," I said.

"Sure. I'll stay here with you in case you need a witness or something," she offered as she began writing in the check book.

"You know Gregory has a master's degree in accounting. If you want, I could see if he would help a couple hours in the afternoon until you find a replacement for Tara," she continued.

In an instant my mood changed back to thankfully happy. How could I loose with my own CPA firm in house? I couldn't say yes soon enough.

"That would be cool with me. Can you see if he'll start today?"

She was as giddy as a school girl as she dialed his number. I half held my breath as I waited to hear the news.

"He'll be here around three-thirty." Just the reply I was hoping for.

"By the way, Tara said she wasn't coming back after lunch. I would have told you earlier, but you were so upset," she added.

I was irritated just a little she hadn't told me earlier, but she seemed so sincere, I figured maybe she was right. It would have been nice to know though.

Just then the phone rang. It was for me. It was a credit card company that informed me I was late on my monthly payment. I explained to the lady on the other end of the phone I did not carry their credit card. She said I had it for the last six months and had been paying my monthly bill online. I told her I never paid online so it was not me. Tara had stolen my identity and had taken out a credit card in my name. Thankfully, it only had a five-hundred-dollar limit. She had maxed it out. I explained to the lady what had happened. She said she did not care; I was still responsible. I said I would pay it and then I wanted it closed. At the time I had perfect credit and did not want to mess it up. Besides, she never picked up her last pay check. I thought that was bad.

I made a police report to Orange Beach Police Department, but nothing happened to her. No wonder there are so many thieves cruising around. The sharks are not the only ones that circle.

The next Monday night was Gregory's boss's Christmas party. After work Barbara said she and her husband, Evan, would pick me up. I thought that was great. The day flew by, and it was time to go home and change for the party. Barbara and Evan lived within two miles of me so I had to change quickly. I heard a horn blow as soon as I had finished getting ready. I walked outside, and it was them. I got in the backseat and buckled up. They were excited that they would get to spend some time with their son and his friend.

When we arrived at the party, we found Gregory and Joshua sitting alone on the quiet side of the room. Barbara motioned for me to take a seat beside Gregory.

"Hi, baby," she said and kissed his cheek.

"Hi, Mama! You look incredible!" he exclaimed.

After a few minutes of idle chitchat, the hostess came near enough for Gregory to flag her down and order wine for the group.

About a glass and a half into the conversation, things shifted to Gregory's work history.

"Sweetheart, tell Wynona about your trip to Turkey," she urged Gregory.

"Well, there's not much to tell. I was the bookkeeper for the International Baptist Mission Board in Istanbul for a couple of years. I was married at the time and living with my three girls. Turkey is a strange place. Have you ever worked overseas, Wynona?" he replied.

"Me? I've traveled to Rome, the Bahamas, St. Croix, and some others places, but it was all for fun—"

"Hi, everyone, I'm Gregory's boss. You must be Barbara and Evan. I'm so glad you made it. Gregory is such a go-getter. I'd even say he's my best employee. I don't know what I'd do without him. Enjoy the party, you guys!" interrupted brunette-butterfly we had been seeing all night.

As the evening wore on, Gregory let me know he was in the market to work in accounting again. He wasn't having a lot of luck in Orange Beach. I didn't want to look like I was trying to steal him away from his current boss so I wished him well with the job hunt. I hated I couldn't just offer him a full-time job.

It was time to head back home to Little Dude, and Gregory offered, instead of Barb. Evan hardly spoke all night, and neither did Joshua.

Two shy guys for sure, I thought as we headed to the parking lot. We got in the truck Gregory was borrowing from Evan.

"Thanks for letting me come to the party, dude. That Joshua sure is a quiet one," I said as I buckled up.

"Sure Wynona. I hope you weren't bored to tears. Joshua has been that way since I met him. He doesn't mean to be that way, but he can't help it," he replied.

"How did you two meet again?" I asked.

"I found him outside of a movie galleria one afternoon a couple of years ago. He didn't know who or where he was. So, I took him in until we found out those answers. His grandmother told me he was in a wreck when he was eighteen and lost his short-term memory."

"Well, do you think it's a good idea to leave him at the party alone?" I asked.

"It's no problem. When I get back, he won't even know I left. Besides, the girls who work with us know what's up. They will watch out for him until I get back," he assured me.

Halfway home, work came up again. I couldn't let him get away.

"Listen, if something ever happens and your mom leaves me, I'd love to hire you full time, but right now, I just can't swing the extra expense."

"No problem. Something will turn up. I'm sure," he said.

Gregory pulled in to let me off at the purple house on the bluff.

"See you on the flip side, dude." I hopped down to my driveway.

As I made my way inside, it was starting to drizzle. I couldn't wait sit down with my feet in front of the fireplace and talk with Little Dude about what he wanted for Christmas.

Business had started picking up, and George saw all the profits. That summer he did not pay me any commissions. I kept calling him asking were my money was. He explained he was keeping it all. He was not going to pay me anymore and I would continue to keep writing insurance for him. I cannot tell you exactly what I said to George, but he got my point. I loaded up Little Dude and went to the bank to close out the accounts. The bank gave me a cashier's check, but it was no use. We had opened up an account under George's Alabama Insurance Agency Inc. name. I was not a member of his corporation; I just didn't want George to steal my clients' premiums. He could take whatever he wanted, and there was nothing I could do about it.

Two officers from the Orange Beach Police Department showed up at my office the next morning.

"Ma'am, are you Wynona?" the older one asked.

"Yes, sir. What can I do for you?"

"George called and filed a theft report with our department. He claims that you removed funds from his trust account. That you have those funds in the form of a cashier's check and have refused to return the funds. Is that true, ma'am?" he said sternly.

"Listen, I was led to believe by George that I was part of the corporation. When he refused to pay my commissions, I knew his next step would be to try and take the clients' premiums that are held in the trust account. I tried to protect my clients by changing banks. I never took the money for myself. The check is in the corporate name, and I still have it. I've been trying to figure out what to do about the problem. I won't let him screw my clients over the way he has me."

"May I see the check?" the officer asked.

I pulled the check from my briefcase and handed it to him. I was as nervous as a Baptist preacher in a brothel. And I was mad enough at George, I could have kicked the skin off his shins.

"Let me call George and see what he wants to do," he said, inspecting the check.

I wondered how long I was going to have to sit in jail until I got someone to post bail for me.

"Hello, this is the Orange Beach Police Department calling. Is this George?"

"I'm glad I caught you. We are here with Wynona. She has placed the check in our custody. What would you like us to do with it?" he asked.

I could hear George yelling something but couldn't make it all out. The officer began to pace back and forth.

"Uh-huh," he said, his face growing red. His pacing became a march.

"Uh-huh. Look George, you can't have it both ways. Either you get the check or I can give it back to Wynona, and I'll take her the station, and you can sign the warrant for her arrest there. Those are your choices, sir. What's it's it going to be?" he demanded. "Fine," he said. He hung up the phone and turned to me, rolling his eyes.

"Am I going to jail?" I asked, my knees knocking.

"I was never going to take you to jail. I had to let George know if anyone was going to put you in jail it was going have to be him. Based on what you already told me, I figured he'd chicken out. I've had enough of that jerk already."

"That makes two of us! So what happens now?" I was still uncertain of my freedom.

"We will turn the check over to him. From there it seems like a civil mater, and we won't be involved further. You have a great day, Wynona." He smiled.

"Well, now that I know I'm not going to the cross-bar hotel, maybe I can." I sighed.

Both headed to the door laughing as they went. All things considered, I didn't have that bad of a day. I was sure relieved that I wouldn't have new sleeping quarters.

The next day at work the bank called. She informed me that George had called her. I was not to write any checks until she cleared it with George first. I explained to her it was not George's money. All the money in the trust account belonged to the clients to pay their insurance premiums. She said she was sorry but it still had to have his approval. I was trying to pay the clients' premiums, and he was still trying to steal their money. You would have thought since I was right, the bank would have helped me out. They did not. Out of the forty thousand, George only approved twenty thousand.

I decided to change my business name to Starfish Insurance Agency and part ways with George for good. I went to a different bank and opened a new trust account for the premiums. I called George up and told him I needed the other twenty thousand to pay the rest of the premiums. He said he did not care; he was keeping the money since I would not write him any more policies. I had to cough up the rest of the cash. It was not my clients' problem I had hooked up with a crook. I paid their premiums, called George, and told him to bite me. I was free.

After I hung up with George, I did what I should have done the day he quit paying my commissions. I looked up the number for the Alabama Insurance Commissioners' office. I explained to the operator that I wanted to make a formal complaint concerning George. She transferred me to the investigator.

"Hi, this is Neal. Can I help you?"

"My name is Wynona. I have a complaint to file against George at Alabama Insurance Agency."

"What exactly is the complaint?"

I explained at length what had transpired between us. Finally, he interrupted me.

"Look, Wynona, I was an agent for ALFA myself, and I know both of you. The department is not going to get involved. I like both of you. Please don't call back on the matter." The phone went silent.

I was beside myself with anger.

The next week I went to a life insurance conference in Birmingham. I stopped for my mid-morning break and called Barbara to see what was going on at the office. She informed me that George was there with an Orange Beach Officer. George said he had a court order that stated that I was to turn over the files to him. I told her no worries. I would call Judge Kevin to see what I could do.

"Hey, Judge Kevin. How could George have a court order to take my files? He doesn't own my company. I'm in Birmingham. Can you help me find out what's going on?"

He started laughing. I didn't find it amusing.

"Don't get stressed out, Wynona. I'll call the officer and get things straightened out. I'll call you back in a second," he reassured me.

I wondered how long it would take at a hundred miles an hour to get to the office so I could throw him out personally. A minute later, the phone rang.

"So what's up?" I asked.

"I asked the officer if he had seen the order. So he asked George for it. All George has is the contract you signed a couple of years ago. I told the officer that he and George were to leave immediately or I'd personally sign the warrant for trespassing." He exploded with laughter.

"Thanks, dude!" I said as I sucked in a breath of fresh air before returning to my seminar.

It had been a long two days. On the drive home, I thought that would be the end of George, but he had me served papers in the next couple of days. I went to see an attorney friend of mine. He said he would take the case and the best thing for me to do was to make copies of the files and mail George a copy. I made the copies and put them in a box to send to George in Birmingham. Before I closed the box, I unwrapped two bags of Tootsie Rolls and laid them on top of the paperwork I had mixed up. Barbara found no humor. Personally that cracked even me up. I mailed it to George, and that was the last I heard from him. I thought life could not get any worse.

I decided I needed some more employees. Barbara and I could not do it all. Gregory and Joshua kept stopping by and taking me to supper after work. We got closer and closer. Gregory became like a brother to me. I trusted him with my life. I hired this young college girl and her aunt. They both checked out. I also decided to move the office in the next two months. I trained them, but they messed up more than they did right. They made the two month mark like the others, then no more. I fired them one day when they came back from lunch. Gregory and Joshua stopped by that afternoon.

"Girl, where the hell is everyone?" he asked, grinning from ear to ear.

"Fired. F.I.R.E.D.!"

"Are you serious?"

"Don't I look serious?" I quipped.

"Yes, you do. Let's get you out of here this afternoon. We'll get cracking tomorrow. How 'bout a few cocktails so you can unwind. My treat?" he offered.

He was right. I was too stressed at that point to concentrate on anything. I needed to vent.

"The best idea I've heard all week. Let's hit it!" I exclaimed.

I grabbed my keys and shut things down. I didn't even feel guilty about it.

Gregory and Joshua were stopping by every day now and working for three hours a day. Gregory said I needed better exposure. He thought I might like to have an office by the toll bridge. I decided it was a good idea and signed a lease. The manager said they would give me a six thousand allowance for a build out. The inside of the office had not been painted, and there was no carpet on the concrete floor. Gregory told me he could do the work for me.

We had only been there about a month when Evan came by to take Barbara to lunch. Little Dude was there because it was summer. He was bored and had been asking me to take him somewhere. Evan overheard Little Dude and asked us to lunch. Little Dude wanted to go so I agreed. We all left and walked the short distance to the nearest hamburger joint. After we were through eating, we started back to the office. At the bottom of the stairwell on the sidewalk was a raised concrete block about six inches tall. It was about two feet long. Barbara was talking to Little Dude and tripped over it. She fell onto the concrete sidewalk. She tried to break the fall with her arms.

"I called an ambulance! It will be here in just a minute," yelled a good Samaritan who saw the fall.

"Thanks!" I told her.

I didn't know if she was being a drama queen or if she was really hurt. The tears streaming down her blouse and the twisted face suggested she was hurt.

"Both of my arms hurt really bad, Evan," she whimpered.

"You're going to be okay. The ambulance is on the way." He pulled out his cell phone and called Gregory. The ambulance pulled in, and she was taken to Foley.

"Meet us at the hospital. Your mom has fallen and is hurt pretty bad," he insisted.

When we arrived at the hospital, we were told that her breaks were severe and she had been transferred to Pensacola.

"We don't all need to go. I'll call you and give you an update when they tell me more," Evan told Gregory.

"Sure, Daddy. Let me know in case I have to take a leave of absence from the furniture store so I can help Wynona," he said.

I had been home from the hospital for about an hour when Gregory called with the news.

"She has twenty-six fractures on one and thirteen on the other. They say she'll been in casts for at least six weeks. Then they say she'll have a long rehab. That sucks!" he stated.

"Dang! I didn't think it was that bad. That does suck."

"She wanted to know if it would be okay if I filled in for her full time until she gets better," he said.

"Sure. I would truly appreciate your help. Thanks so much!"

"Cool. I'll be there first thing in the morning, chick! Later!"

I was relieved. He knew the system and had a master's in accounting. He might even be better at the job than his mom. Barbara never did come back.

MY NEW BEST FRIENDS

Gregory was filling in for Barbara better than I had hoped. Joshua was, to great surprise, serving as my receptionist. I never would have known he had memory problems. For the first time in years, my appointment book was flawless. I was able to focus my efforts on selling, and things were rolling along like a locomotive. I decided to hire another person. I put a help-wanted AD in the local paper. This time the first applicant was a young college girl, still wet behind the ears from some sorority. She seemed bright enough, even broke the blonde stereotype bearing some intelligence, so I hired her. She had a cousin from Mississippi with accounting experience from her limited work in the casino industry, so I hired her as well. The next day they began their employment with my little firm. I knew that they needed immediate training so day one began insurance boot camp 101. After a week's worth of barking orders, the girls had what I thought they needed to know at that point so I backed off the reigns and let them take a few steps on their own.

Months in I was becoming tired of the constant corrections I was making. I didn't feel that more training would help. They just didn't get it so out the door they went.

Soon Christmas arrived, and Orange Beach glowed with lights on ever pole. Good cheer was in the air. Little Dude had already made his long list for Santa Claus. He decided he had been a real good Little Dude this year. I agreed.

As the days rolled on, Gregory and I got closer, like brother and sister. He called me one day to invite me and Little Dude to his parents' family Christmas dinner. Christmas Eve finally came. Little Dude and I loaded up in the H2. It was only a two-mile ride to his parents' house in Orange Beach. On the way I got my first present of the season in the form a speeding ticket.

Little Dude was still laughing as we pulled into Barbara and Evan's driveway. Gregory heard us pull up and came outside. Gregory came up to us and asked what's up. Little Dude explained what had happened. Then everyone was laughing as we walked inside. There we found Barbara, Evan, and Gregory's sister, Joy. When Gregory told them what happened, they all started laughing. We went to the table to eat.

They had two tables set up on the enclosed porch so we could see the sunset. The sunroom had nothing but windows. Gregory made sure that Little Dude and I sat at the table with him and Joshua. We had turkey and dressing and all the fixings that go with it. Afterward everyone had cake but Little Dude. He wanted ice cream, which he got. When we were all finished, we got up to go to the living room to open presents. Little Dude's Christmas card came with twenty dollars and a Ziploc bag full of marshmallows. The night ended, and it was time to go home. It had been a wonderful night.

On Christmas Day, Little Dude and I loaded up to go to Mom's house. It was a cold and cloudy day. When we arrived in Josephine, we found the Christmas spirit to be alive. You could see Christmas trees lit up inside of people's houses in Stone Quarry where Mom lived. It was beautiful. We pulled into Mom's drive. I had barely stopped the car when Little Dude opened the door. He flew inside to see what was there. Baby Doll and her family, and Chickee and her family were already inside. Dinner was ready and about to be served. We all sat down in the dining room to eat. It was turkey and dressing, potatoes, green beans, tomatoes, and just about anything else you could think of. After everyone got stuffed, we got up to go to the living room, and Baby Doll started giving out the presents. Mom and the kids were pleased. No one else got one, which was fine. I had a bad habit of buying from me to me at Christmas, so I was cool. It finally came to an end, and it was time to go home. Little Dude was so tired he slept all the way to the purple house on the bluff. It had been a good Christmas.

As the days rolled into weeks and weeks into months, it was finally summertime. During one of our afternoon chitchat sessions one day, Gregory floored me.

"Mom won her lawsuit against the management company where she fell." He was gloating.

"What lawsuit?"

"Well, they wouldn't pay her medical bills so she got a lawyer and sued them."

"I thought your mom had insurance and that they paid her bills."

"They did. But her attorney figured a way to make them pay the insurance company back and mom's deductible, plus they got extra money for her pain and suffering. We're going out tonight to celebrate. Mom and dad said they had a surprise lined up. I can't wait to find out what it is!" He hit the door almost running as he left.

I couldn't help but think how lawyers screw everyone they can. I wondered how much they had gotten, but Gregory left in such a hurry, I didn't get the chance to ask.

The next day was Saturday, and I went to the office to see who I had meetings with. Gregory and Joshua burst through the office door holding hands and giggling like school girls. I tried to make sense of what I was seeing but was interrupted.

"You gotta come out side and see what they bought me, Wynona!" Gregory insisted as he grabbed me by the arm. They dragged me to the parking lot and pointed at a brand new Porsche Spyder. My jaw was on the sidewalk.

"You have to be kidding me!" I admired the little silver convertible.

"Mom bought me and sis one. They are so cool."

I guess he was caught up in the moment because he and Joshua were still holding hands.

"So, does your mom know?" I inquired.

"Know what?" He looked puzzled.

"About you and Joshua."

He let go of his hand and looked at me for a few moments. The look of joy and jubilation turned into embarrassment.

"Mom's in denial. She has a hard time accepting that I was once married with kids and now I'm with a man. Are you okay with it?" He shifted uncomfortably.

"I knew you would turn out to be either married still or gay. All the good ones are!" I laughed.

"Well, sweetie, if I met you before Joshua, I'd still be straight." He winked.

About a month later, Gregory said it fun driving around town but it had no trunk room. Gregory explained that when he mentioned it to Barbara, she and Evan threw a fit. They told him if he wanted something else he would have to go buy it himself. He asked me if I would take them to look at a Jeep because they have more room.

We got in the H2 and headed to Foley to a local dealership. The owner was a good friend of mine, Doug. Through the years, I bought a lot of cars from him. He always told me straight up. My kind of dude.

When we arrived, Doug was in the lobby. He walked slowly over and gave me a big bear hug. His employees looked at me like they had been shot. Doug did not do that to just anybody. We were tight even though sometimes it would be years before we saw each other or talked. After we all said hello, Doug turned us over to a salesperson named Craig. Craig took us out to the car lot to see what they had. We headed for the Jeeps. What a nice selection they had. Gregory and Joshua walked around looking. I got tired of standing and pointed to a green, four-door one. Joshua said that was fine, but Gregory said no. I turned and looked at Gregory and told him that was it. I was tired and ready to go home to the purple house on the bluff. Gregory had a sad look on his face as he said okay. We walked inside to see the finance manager who was also a friend of mine. He gave me a hug and shook Gregory and Joshua's hand.

"I have bad credit, and we would really like to buy the Jeep we just looked at. If you can get me financed, I'll buy it right now," he told him.

"What about him?" He pointed to Joshua.

"He doesn't have any credit at all. Can you still help?"

After running his credit report, the finance manager looked up and shook his head. "Without a good cosigner, there's nothing I can do."

Dejected, he turned to me.

"Wynona, would you cosign with Joshua. It would really help us out and help build his credit. You know we're good for it and won't screw you over," he begged.

"Sure," I agreed before I could remember my dad's warning about such things.

Even with me as a cosigner, the finance manager let them know they still had to come up with the five-thousand-dollar down payment.

"We can pay it back every week. You can keep a hundred dollars from each of us till we pay you back."

I began writing the check without a second thought.

As I headed home to Little Dude, I thought about how Gregory had become like a brother and how lucky I was to have his friendship. Barbara and Evan kept in touch after the fall and sometimes babysat for me from time to time. All of my time was spent selling, selling, selling!

One day Barbara called the office to let me know they had rented a condo on the beach. She told me they also rented a pontoon boat with a slide so Little Dude could have some fun while I slaved away at work. That night I ran it by him. He was like a rubber ball bouncing off the walls with excitement. He left for a few minutes then came back with his bag packed. We finally found a cure for his boredom.

The next day I drove him the short jaunt to the condo to make sure it wasn't rickety or dangerous. It was impressive. It had its own tiki bar beside two out-of-this-world pools with fountains and waterfalls. The boat they rented was anchored in the private harbor behind the condo. I thanked them for letting him come hang out and headed to work. Little Dude was way too excited. He was the only child there and got all the attention. After four nights the little vacation was over. Reluctantly he came back home. I couldn't blame him. I was in need of a vacation myself.

A couple of weeks later, after working ten to twelve hours a day, Gregory turned and looked at me. He said it would be nice to take Little Dude on a Mexican cruise out of Mobile, Alabama. I decided not only would I take Little Dude, I'd offer them a bonus and pay for them to go as well. They agreed, and I booked us a four-night and five-day cruise. I got home that night after work to tell Little Dude the good news. He immediately raced for his suitcase to start packing even though the cruise was three weeks away. I also booked us two rooms in Mobile at a nice motel across the street from the cruise ship terminal for the night before we departed.

The day finally arrived for us to go to Mobile. During boarding Little Dude bounced up and down the gang plank. What an adventure we had. We swam with the dolphins in Cozumel, and he body surfed the waves in Cancun. We took in a show with Little Dude every night after dinner. He was the perfect gentleman. Gregory and Joshua would hit the casinos afterward. Too quickly the trip ended. We all had a great time.

As the summer ended, my only regret was Little Dude would be back at school and our fun time would be limited again. At work, even though we were short-handed, I didn't even consider hiring anymore help. We were a well-oiled machine.

THE BAPTISM

Late in November I was engrossed in my work when Joshua announced that Pastor Roy was on the line for me. I immediately felt guilty.

"Wynona, you haven't been in church the last two Sundays in a row. I was just wondering why."

I always sat in different places so he wouldn't know when I skipped services.

"How do you know that, Pastor Roy?" I asked.

"I keep up with you. Trust me. I know." He laughed.

"Well, I was sick last Sunday, and the week before I was out of town."

"Okay. I'll see you this Sunday then, right?"

"Yes, sir. Only I'm not going to tell you where I'll sit!" I laughed.

I was so glad to have a good pastor like Pastor Roy. I began to reflect on my life and God. Soon I was daydreaming about a trip I took to Hawaii several years earlier when I worked for ALFA.

During my employment, they gave me opportunities to win two trips a year. One was called the All-Star and was for the families. It was always at Disney World, Williamsburg, and places like that. The other was called the Super Star. It was for adults and children sixteen years and older. Little Dude was too young to go on the Super Star trips. Those were always exceptional. I won a trip to Rome, Italy, a couple of cruises, and, the one I remember the most, Maui, Hawaii. At the time I won the trip, I was single and between husbands so I decided to take my girlfriend Sherry.

The day finally arrived for me and Sherry to load up and cruise to Montgomery, Alabama. That was where we were to catch the chartered flight with the other ALFA Insurance Company agents. We left the day before our flight was to leave to spend the night close to the airport in case we had any car problems. I picked Sherry up at her house, and off we went. We were so excited. Sherry had been to Hawaii once before on her honeymoon, and I had never been. We arrived safely in Montgomery and checked in the hotel for the one-night stay.

The next day we awoke to a hot, sunny day, ready for our big adventure. Since it was a private flight, there was no wait. The airport was nothing like a regional airport—nothing special. The terminal was on the ground. The airport employees had to roll a set of stairs up to the airplane door for everyone to get in. I thought, *This redneck is reliving the seventies.* The airplane was full, and we finally took off. It was a long flight but a smooth one. We landed safely in Hawaii and got off the plane to get on the chartered buses to cruise the short drive to the hotel. Was that place ever nice. It was huge, like being in a castle. The lobby looked like something out of a movie. It had potted palm trees all through the lobby. The double doors facing the ocean were open, letting the tropical breeze blow through, cooling everyone off.

We checked in with no worries, dropped our luggage, and were off to go and explore the hotel before we went to the welcome dinner. We found the pool, the beach, the hotel shops, and the restaurants and bars. The sun was setting on the horizon as we walked the short distance to dinner. They had an open bar and a buffet. We ate and had a cocktail then decided to hang out at the hotel bar so we would be fresh for the next day and what memories laid ahead.

Sherry did not let me sleep past seven o'clock. I was on vacation and had to get up early like I would to go to work. When we finally got up and had breakfast, we decided to go into town and play tourist. We called a taxi and went to the tourist strip. We had a real nice lunch at a restaurant that was built over the ocean. It had no air conditioner. Instead it was completely open to let the tropical breeze blow through. We saw plenty of boats and surfer dudes. We went shopping and paid too much for thirsts and souvenirs just to have something that said "Hawaii." That was all we did that week until we decided to rent a convertible the day before we were to head home. Sherry wanted to go to the top of the mountain to see the seven sacred pools. Looking back, a postcard of the falls would have done just fine.

We caught a ride to the rental place with one of my bosses. Sherry and I tried to talk him into coming with us to the falls, but he declined. We grabbed the keys from the rental desk to the Sebring convertible and headed out. Sherry drove since she had been on the island before and knew the way. We started down the four-lane highway and took in the beautiful view. After being on the road for about an hour, we decided to stop in a tiny little town for lunch. At this shanty, we found what could only be described as the most beautiful view of the island we had seen. The place didn't have glass windows or even a door, but they laid out the tastiest tuna I have ever eaten. Thirty minutes after we sat down for lunch, our bellies were full, and we were back on our adventure trail. The road went from four lanes to two right outside of town, and civilization thinned. The one-and-a-half-lane road had fifty-one one-lane bridges and 161 curves. The curves were breakneck, switch-back roads, nothing like back home. Every time we came to a curve, we had to stop and blow the horn to keep from running head-on into oncoming traffic. You couldn't see around the curve, and on one side of the road was a three-thousand-foot plunge. No guard rails, just a couple of reflectors in the pavement near the edge. In what they considered dangerous turns, they had three-feet-tall and six-feet-long brick walls.

We crept up the narrow pig trail and finally made it after about two hours of white-knuckle driving. When we arrived, we watched the first of many cliff divers taking the plunge into the pond of water below. Sherry and I didn't bring our suits, we decided not to go swimming and just watched the fun. We had had enough after an hour and got back in the convertible and headed back down the mountain.

You may not believe in God, but what happened next was nothing short of a miracle.

Every once in a while, I would feel a couple of bumps, and I realized what those blue reflectors we had seen meant. Everyone she hit got a request from me to get back on the road, preferably somewhere in the middle. She always responded the same way, saying that she didn't want to hit anyone head-on. I told her if she didn't pay attention we wouldn't have to worry about it because we would be dead at the bottom of the cliff. We had packed an ice chest with a twelve pack of beer. Sherry was making me so nervous, I popped two for us to have on the ride down. I handed her a beer and reached to get a smoke from my purse. That's when I heard the screeching of what I thought was a crane. The sound was coming from the steel of the car's bottom scraping the top of the retaining wall as two tires climbed onto the very top. I was curled up into a ball when I heard Sherry scream. I turned to look and saw her shaking as she gripped the steering wheel with. It seemed like minutes but turned out to be seconds when we finished riding the wall. God gently sat us down in our lane, and oncoming traffic raced by us.

I spotted a place to pull over. We sat there with two flat tires and were more shaken than a martini. Finally, with the help of some good Samaritans, we managed to get off the mountain alive.

Sherry and I went to the company dinner that night. When we arrived we found out we were the buzz of conversation. All we heard about was the accident and the miracle that had happened. It had been a long day. The next day we were flying home to Alabama. We could hardly wait to get off that island.

I just knew that God had saved me on that mountain for a reason.

I awoke from my daydream, and I immediately picked the phone back up and called Pastor Roy.

"I know you weren't expecting my call, but I've been thinking it would be a good time for me to rededicate my life to Christ."

"That's great news, Wynona! Come by my office next week, and we can talk about it then. Again, great news!" he said.

I went to church to film my part for the baptism. After I was finished, he said that was perfect.

The following Sunday was the big day. My mom, Little Dude, Baby Doll and her family, Chickee and her family, and Barbara and Evan came to show their support.

After announcements, Pastor Roy told the congregation to look at one of the three TVs that were located on the front wall of the church. There were four people in front of me that told their story. I was the last in line.

The baptism began, and the room fell silent. The ones before me had no worries getting in and out of the small pool. It was finally my turn. I walked to the steps leading to the pool. I was about to step in the pool when I felt a gentle shove from behind. I looked around, but there was no one there. I guess God had waited long enough and was saying, "Get her done." I stepped into the pool and sat down. Pastor Roy asked me to state my name. Pastor Roy started laughing and told the congregation just to call me Wynona. Everyone laughed. It cracked me up, too. When you have been married three times, you may as well just go by your first name. Pastor Roy said his piece and dipped me under the water. He helped me out of the pool, and again I felt a gentle shove. This time I did not look around because I knew no one was there but the Holy Spirit.

I went back to change into some dry clothes. I found my family and sat down by Little Dude. He just looked at me with those pretty, baby blue eyes and said everyone had been laughing at me. I let him know it was okay. They were not laughing at me but with me. It never hurt to put a smile on someone's face, especially in these hard times. People were losing their jobs, their houses, their cars. I was glad to know that I could put a smile on some faces that had not smiled about much in a long time.

After church ended, Mom, Little Dude, and I walked to the car. The mayor of Gulf Shores stopped us on the sidewalk. He had been a friend of the family for years. Mayor David's dad sold a house to my parents when I was in elementary school. Mayor David never forgot the kindness and friendship my parents had shown his. He shook my hand and told me he was proud of me. I thought that was one of the best compliments I could have received. I thanked him, and we left.

That day I felt a peace within me. I knew now that my life would be filled without worries. God was preparing me for what would happen in the days ahead. He wanted me to know he was there for me like he had always been. I had not always been there for him. Now I had a new look on life and was ready for whatever lay ahead.

NEIGHBORS

Gregory, Joshua, and I worked ten-hour days. Afterward we would always go out for dinner and drinks. I would always pay to show them my appreciation. They always seemed to appreciate it.

We worked harder than normal for several months straight. It was now wintertime, and the island had turned into a ghost town. I was tired. I needed a break. I thought about where Little Dude would like to go on vacation. I finally decided to take him to Florida for the weekend to swim the manatees. We were there the year before, and even though it was only for the weekend, it had been one of the most relaxing vacations I had ever been on.

I asked Gregory and Joshua if they wanted to go. Gregory said no, that they had plans and someone had to stay behind to feed my eight dogs. I liked that about him; he always knew exactly how to help me. Little Dude and I went on the trip with the local dive shop. We stayed in an old hotel on the water. We went swimming with the manatees all day and met for dinner at night. The weekend flew by, and it was time to pack and go home.

🌿

The day after we got home, I dropped Little Dude off at school and headed for work.

Gregory and Joshua were already there. Joshua made me a pot of coffee. I poured myself a cup and sat down at my desk.

"So how did the weekend go, Gregory?"

"Everything was just fine, sweetie."

"Any trouble with the dogs or the house?"

"No, they were their usual, playful selves, and the house is still standing." He winked.

It was nice to have a friend like him. *It's a shame he's gay*, I thought.

When Little Dude got out of school that day, I picked him up and headed home to the purple house. It had been a long drive back the day before and I was still tired. As the afternoon sun was setting, I was sitting outside on my wrap-around porch when I noticed two set of car lights coming down the driveway. I wondered who it could be since nobody ever came to see me unless they called me first. When they pulled up to the house it was two Orange Beach Police officers. They got out of their cars and walked over to me.

"What can I do for you gentlemen?"

"Ma'am you are being given a citation for dogs at large. You are Wynona, correct?"

"I am Wynona, but I never let my dogs run wild. My dogs stay in that pen, except when I feed them and they are inside with me at night when I'm watching television. I don't know what you're talking about. But give me the ticket, and I'll take care of it immediately."

He handed me the ridiculous ticket and explained that I could face six months jail time and a five-hundred-dollar fine for each complaint.

"Look, I was on a trip this weekend, and as far as I know, the dogs didn't get out. They were in their pen, like they are now when I got home just a little while ago."

"That's good to hear, ma'am. Have a good evening."

As their tail lights were disappearing, I began dialing Gregory's cell. It rang until his voice mail picked up. I just hung up. I made my way back to the porch, and the phone rang. It was Gregory.

"Hey, Wynona, what's up? Is everything okay?"

"What's up? I just got a ticket for dogs at Large. I thought you said everything was fine this weekend. Did they get out, or what?"

"I swear they were in the pen all weekend. I didn't even let them out when we fed them because we were in a hurry to go see Joshua's mom."

"All right."

"Do you think someone in the neighborhood is just being a jackass?"

"I don't know, dude. I hope not. See you tomorrow."

We were swamped at work, and the days flew into weeks. The next thing I knew it was time for spring break. Little Dude and I had been going to Ft. Walton

Beach, Florida, every year. I had already made the reservation at a motel. It had a huge pool that connected to the room on the bottom floor. Our room was one of them. Little Dude just loved it, and I did, too. I didn't have to haul his floats all over the place, and I could sit on the deck by the pool and watch him swim. We spent our week at the pool, going to the beach, and to dinner. I kept in touch with Gregory the whole week to see how the dogs were doing and what was going on at work. He said everything was fine. The nights we did not go out to dinner we ordered room service. I think of all the things Little Dude loved to do, ordering room service was his favorite. Yikes! The bill wasn't my favorite. I paid fifteen bucks for chicken fingers and fries each. The week finally ended, and we loaded up for the two-hour drive home.

We pulled up in the yard, and I noticed a piece of paper taped to the door. I let Little Dude out so he could go inside to watch a cartoon. I pulled the paper off the door. To my surprise, it was another citation for dogs at large. I thought it was absurd so I threw it in the trash. I dialed Gregory's number.

"I'll give you two guesses as to why I called you."

"Did your hot-water heater leak again?"

"Bzzt! Nope. I got another dogs at large ticket, dude. Swear to me that the dogs didn't get out. And if they did, let me know now. Cool?"

"I swear it, Wynona. You know I would tell you if they got out. Someone in your neighborhood really has it in for you chick is all I can suggest."

I was too busy to have to deal with crap like this so I blew it off.

🌿

One of the companies I sold insurance for was AGLA; they sold life insurance in forty-eight states. I was a special representative for the company. I did not have to go to any of the meetings but still had the opportunity to win trips. That year they had a trip to Cancun, Mexico. Out of thousands of agents, I was number one. I was the only special rep they had that won that year. It was to an all-exclusive resort on the beach. Little Dude and I were both thrilled. We had been to Mexico plenty of times but never stayed at a resort like that. The trip was that summer. Time was passing like it does on a bad date. We were ready to go, but it was nowhere near the departure date.

A dear friend from high school tragically lost one of her daughters. I wanted to do something to help take their mind off of things for a while and invited them to join us on the trip to Cancun. You would have thought they just won the big Powerball or something when I asked them. About a month later, the departure date snuck up on us.

Flying into Cancun was breathtaking. The water was so blue and clear. The hotel was definitely all they said it was. The only thing it didn't have was a gold brick road. We went sight seeing and souvenirs shopping half the time. The other half we sat poolside and just soaked up the good life for a while. Five nights just isn't enough time to enjoy paradise. I would have stayed a month if I could have figured out a way. But duty called. I waited until the last second to pack, just to get in a few more minutes. The plane ride home let me know I was beat. I slept the whole way.

The next morning I slept a little late, even though I needed to be at work. I made some coffee to get ready for a busy day at work. Little Dude woke up and wanted some breakfast. I cooked eggs for him and poured me a cup of coffee. He ate and I sat there and watched the news. I got up to get another cup when Little Dude yelled at me someone was here. I got my coffee and walked to the front door. I stepped out on the porch and saw two Orange Beach cop cars parked in front of my house. They got out of their cars and walked over to me. My friend Chris stepped out of one car. He came up to me with a sad look on his face.

"What's with the sad sack face, Chris?"

He handed me another dogs at large ticket. Now I was the one with sad sack face.

"I'm sorry, Wynona. You know we are just doing our job. Give the clerk a call, and she'll give you the court date and where it's going to be held."

What a surprise, I thought as they left. So that's three. I could get a year and a half in the jail and have to pay fifteen hundred bucks for nothing. I walked around the yard trying to get a signal so I could call Gregory.

"Dude, you aren't going to believe it. It happened again. I got another ticket for you-know-what."

I must have walked in an ant bed because about ten of them were biting my toes.

"Say it isn't true!"

"Oh, it's true all right. Did you see or talk to anyone who you can think might be behind this crap?"

"We didn't. No one said anything to us or anything. I wish I could help, chick."

I wasn't worried, just pissed. I could prove I was gone every time they claimed the dogs were out. Gregory wouldn't lie, especially over something so stupid. I dialed the clerk's office at city hall.

"Hey, girl, how are you doing?" I asked my girlfriend in the clerk's office.

"Wynona! What's shaking?"

"I got some tickets for dogs at large, and Chris told me to call you and get the court date."

I could hear someone whisper in her ear as she tried to mute the receiver.

"Susan just told me that she has paperwork to issue an arrest warrant on you."

"You can't be serious."

"It's just waiting for the judge to sign."

"Screw it. I'll just come down now and turn myself in. I'm ready to get the crap resolved. See you in a few."

I hung up. Mad is only one tenth of the rage I felt. I asked Gregory to come by and give me a lift in case they booked me.

He drove me the short distance to the police department, and we got out and went inside. I pushed the little button and explained to the dispatcher what I was doing there. He said he would send an officer right on out. A few minutes later Chris showed up and told me to follow him to the back. Gregory stood up to go with me. Chris just looked at him and told him to sit back down, so he did.

When Chris and I got to the back, we sat down at his desk. He looked at me and let me know he felt uncomfortable taking the report since we were friends.

"Is it okay if another officer takes your statement?"

"No worries."

He walked over to another officer sitting near us and motioned for him to take care of me.

"Do you have to lock me up?" I asked the officer as he sat down.

He laughed out loud and took my statement.

"You don't have to go to jail now, but if you don't show up for court, they will issue a bench warrant for you. So don't miss your court date."

"Don't worry about me. I'll be there so I can clear my name. Bank on it."

I shot up out of the chair I was sitting in and made a bee-line for the exit to collect Gregory. He looked shocked when I rounded the corner sporting a huge smile. Who ever was messing with me was going to have to face me in court and tell the same lies.

A month later it was time for court. Gregory and Joshua wanted to go with me to show support. We left work and went straight to the courthouse. When we arrived, I checked in with the city clerk and took a seat in the courtroom. Judge Buck walked in and took his seat in the front. They took the prisoners in the orange jumpsuits first. It said on there back property of the city of Orange Beach. The cases continued as I patiently waited my turn, and then I heard my name called. I started walking to the front when I noticed the neighbors across the street walking to the front with me. It was Ruby and his wife, Susan. I was shocked. I thought we were friends. She had her chin stuck out past her nose as she strutted toward the prosecution table. She didn't even look at me as we waited for the judge to begin.

We stood before Judge Buck, not saying a word. Judge Buck looked at everyone then began. "Wynona is a friend of mine and also a client. I do not feel comfortable sitting on this case. I am moving it to Summerdale."

Susan threw her hands on her three-hundred-pound hip.

"Oh-no you don't. You are going to try this case right here and now. I've waited long enough!"

Judge Buck leaned over his desk and looked her dead in the eyes. I thought he may actually jump over his desk at her when he began shaking his index finger at her.

"I guess you didn't hear me the first time! I said I'm not trying this case! Please don't make me repeat myself again. Got it? Wynona, is that okay with you?"

"Yes, sir. Whatever is good with you is good with me. You're the judge."

He looked at everyone one more time. He held his eyes on the docket as he spoke.

"The case will be heard next month in Summerdale."

Smack! His gavel hit the desk, and we got to leave.

I was standing outside with Gregory and Joshua smoking a cigarette. Susan came outside and started walking toward her car. All of a sudden, Gregory started yelling at her, "It is not her fault! You're making all this up!" I felt a tap on my shoulder. It was my attorney. He told me not to say a word. So I didn't. Gregory kept yelling at her.

Susan finally yelled back, "I am not being mean! I am worried about my children. Her dogs have tried to bite them three times!" Gregory, Joshua, and I got in the truck to go to the purple house. What a day.

A month later it was time for court. Gregory, Joshua, and I loaded up to cruise to Summerdale. When we arrived and walked inside, I found the courtroom to be packed. Gregory and Joshua sat down while I went to check in. I was standing there waiting my turn when the city clerk of Orange Beach walked up to me. She said she had my back and to go sit down, so I did. Minutes later, court started. The judge was young and one I did not know. There were a few cases in front of me. While waiting, the city prosecutor went over and whispered something in Susan's ear. She and her husband stood up and followed the prosecutor outside. Gregory could not stand it. He leaned over and told me he was going outside to smoke a cigarette.

When he came back a few minutes later, he was smiling.

"They told her to go home, Wynona."

"What?"

"For real. The prosecutor told her that it had been decided that nothing was going to happen to you so she might as well leave."

"Sweet."

Next they called my case. I walked up front with my attorney. The prosecutor was already standing up front waiting on us.

"I understand you have a recommendation in this case, Mr. Prosecutor."

"We do, Your Honor. We recommend doggy probation instead of any jail time or fines."

"Wynona, if you don't get another ticket in the next twelve months, this will all go away. Now, pay the clerk, and have a nice day. Next case."

What a relief. I still wasn't satisfied, though. I didn't get to clear my name, but at least it was over. I still didn't know what motivated Susan to do this to me. Gregory suggested she was jealous of my success. Who knows. The purple house called me home.

Two months had passed with nothing very exciting happening. Gregory, Joshua, and I were busy at work. Gregory always raced me to answer the phone. Every time I answered it, he got a little nervous. When I did get to answer the phone, he listened to every word that was said. I started feeling a little overprotected. I figured I just needed a break and took Little Dude to the penthouse for the weekend.

One afternoon the next week, Little Dude was inside watching a movie, and I was sitting on the porch unwinding from a long day at the office. I heard a car coming down my long driveway. I looked up to see two sets of headlights. This time I knew what it meant. Sure enough, it was two Orange Beach Officers that I did not know. They parked their cars and got out. They walked up to me. I said, "Hi, dude, what's up?"

"We heard you were collecting these." He handed me my fourth ticket.

"Yuck, yuck." I said sarcastically.

Court was going to be in Summerdale the next month. I dialed Gregory's number.

"Got another one, dude."

"You don't mean a ticket for the dogs, do you?"

"What else. I'm so sick of this. I mean, I leave, and she calls the law. This is really pissing me off."

"Don't do anything crazy. You don't need to go to jail for assault."

"No worries. See you at work in the morning."

I still couldn't figure out why Susan was being so mean. I was glad Gregory was so supportive.

The following month the court date arrived. Gregory, Joshua, and I loaded up in the H2 to go back to Summerdale. When we arrived, we found court to be packed. This time I walked in and waved to the city clerk. Instead of getting in the long line, we took a seat.

Court was supposed to start at four. The judge finally showed up at five thirty. He came in and sat down front. He apologized for being late and did a short spiel about hats and cell phones. He looked at the city clerk and asked her who the first case was. To my surprise, they called my name. I had never been to court where I got to go in front of the inmates.

The judge looked at the prosecutor and asked him what he recommended. He said all he wanted to do was extend Nona's doggy probation for an additional six months. The judge agreed. About that time, the city clerk piped up. She looked at the judge and wanted to know what he wanted to do with my first two tickets. The prosecutor spoke up and said he would just let those two go away.

Because I got in trouble again while on probation, I was supposed to get up to two years in jail and up to two thousand in fines plus court costs. The judge agreed and told me to pay court cost and be on my way. I paid, and Gregory, Joshua, and I got in the truck to go to dinner. That night Gregory seemed distant I thought he would be thrilled for my victory. Instead he just stared into his food. I asked him if he was feeling well. He said no, that he felt like he had the flu.

The next day it was back to work. That was on a Friday. I had Little Dude for the weekend and was looking forward to doing something fun. While driving down the road, he looked at me and asked me if it was okay if he went to live with his dad for a while. I was disappointed but told him yes. That Sunday, I packed his little suitcase and dropped him off at his dad's. I went home to get a good night's rest for work the next day.

The next morning Gregory and Joshua came over before work to feed my dogs. I told them about Little Dude going to his dad's for a while the night before. It was their way of showing me some support, I guess. They even brought me a cup of coffee from the gas station down the street. Lucky for me, too, because I had forgotten to get my coffee-maker going in the rush to get ready. That became our new routine—feed dogs, drink coffee, and then off to work. It felt comfortable. I felt loved.

THE ROUTINE

It was spring now, and every day started out pretty much the same. Gregory and Joshua would come over every morning to feed my dogs and bring me a cup of coffee. They even started doing it on the weekends, which was something new for them. How happy I was that they loved me so much, they wanted to spend more time helping me.

After about two weeks of the new routine, I became deathly sick. There was a bug going around town, and I had gotten it. After a couple of days of vomiting, I decided I needed to go see my family doctor. I called Gregory and asked him to pick me up and take me to see Dr. Ned. About thirty minutes passed, and there was a knock on my door. Gregory and Joshua were standing there with my cup of coffee. It took all my energy to go outside on the porch to sit with them.

Gregory asked me, "How are you doing?"

"I'm fine, just a little under the weather." He smiled and gave me the coffee. "I really don't feel like drinking it right now," I said.

"Come on. It will make you feel better and wake you up," Gregory said. I felt like death warmed over as I sat there with them and drank it. They stayed until I finished mine, and then they went to go feed the dogs. On the way back to the car, I told Gregory to come look at my arm. I had two red bumps on my forearm that looked like a really weird boil.

"Do you have any idea what these bumps are?" I asked.

"Wynona, those are spider bites. I'll go open the office and come back around ten and take you to Dr. Ned's office in Foley," he said.

"Okay, but call me on your way here so you can make sure I'm awake." At the time all I did was sleep and stagger to the bathroom.

I crawled back in bed and went to sleep. It seemed like only minutes but had been a couple of hours when the cell phone rang. I answered, and it was Gregory. He and Joshua were leaving the office to pick me up. I slowly got out of bed to get dressed. I was so tired, I only took three short steps before I had to stop and rest. What should have only taken me five minutes to do ended up taking thirty.

About the time I finished dressing, there was a knock on the door.

I yelled, "Come in!" It was Gregory and Joshua with another cup of coffee. They put me in the Jeep and headed to the doctor's office. I was feeling even worse since the second cup of coffee I had.

The nurse took me to the back and sat me in a chair in the exam room as soon as I arrived. A few minutes later Dr. Ned came in.

"What brings you here today, Wynona?"

"I feel like I have the flu, and I think I have some spider bites on my arm."

"I think you're right. Let me get you a script for it, and you will be good as new in a few days."

He wrote me a prescription for an antibiotic. Gregory, Joshua, and I left his office to go to the drugstore and get it filled.

The drugstore I used was located right beside the office. We went to the drive-up window.

"How long will it take?" Gregory asked.

"About twenty minutes."

"Cool. Wynona, what do you want to do?"

"Go to the office, and let me check my messages."

"I don't think that's a good idea. You can barely hold your head up!"

"No worries. I am going, so start driving."

Reluctantly he did, and we parked in front of the office and went inside. It was nice to be back. I missed talking to the clients and making money. I looked and felt like crap, but at last I was doing my thing.

While we were there, Gregory kept answering the phone, telling me, "It's just busy work. Only mortgage companies wanting proof of insurance. I can handle it since I have your signature stamp."

The twenty minutes seemed like hours, but finally it was time to get my medicine. We loaded up in the Jeep and went back to the drive-up window. We got my medicine and cruised back to the purple house. Gregory took me inside and put me in bed. He got me a glass of water since that was all I could keep down and gave me a pill to take. I just hoped that in two or three days I would be fine and back to work.

The next morning Gregory and Joshua came to the purple house to feed my dogs and bring my cup of coffee. This time I did not feel like drinking it so I sat it down by my chair on the porch.

"Hey, why aren't you drinking your coffee?" Gregory asked after some time had gone by.

"Because I don't feel like praying to the porcelain queen. It would be easier for me if you would make me a pot here in the mornings when you come over."

"It's easier on me, Wynona, if I just stop at the store and buy you a cup. I don't think I have time to make you one here."

I could not argue with him since I had to run to the bathroom again.

In the days that followed, nothing would stay down except for a few crackers and a glass of water. A month went by, and I was not feeling any better.

"I need to go back to Dr. Ned and get a different antibiotic," I said to Gregory one morning.

"Make the appointment, and I'll drive you."

After I made the appointment, I called Gregory and told him the time.

"Okay, sweetie, I'll call you when I'm leaving the office to wake you up." At that time, out of twenty-four hours, I slept for twenty-three. I would wake up three or four times a day and would only stay awake ten to fifteen minutes. I felt like I'd wake up at anytime and see the Grim Reaper standing at the foot of my bed.

Gregory called hours later to let me know that he and Joshua were on their way. I got out of bed and got ready. They picked me up, and back to Foley we went. I checked in when I arrived and immediately heard my name called. The nurse was standing at the door telling me to come on back. I went into the same small room. The door was open, and Dr. Ned was sitting there waiting on me.

"Didn't I just see you a couple of weeks ago? What's going on with you this time?" he asked.

"The antibiotic is not working, and I need something else." This time I showed him the purple marks that had been popping up on my arms. "What can these be?"

"I'm not sure, but they look like some kind of insect bites."

"I've been bitten by a lot of things, but they never looked like this, Dr. Ned. If that's what you think they are, is there some stronger antibiotic that will help?"

"Sure. Let me get my pad." He scribbled something down then handed me the piece of paper. "Let me know if you have any more problems."

After we picked up the new antibiotic, Gregory drove me back home, put me to bed, and gave me a pill to take. They left, and I went back to sleep. It seemed like my life was passing me by, and I had no control.

The next morning I woke up to find Gregory and Joshua standing beside my bed.

"How did you get in?"

"I know the combination to the lock on the living room door," Gregory said.

He gave me my morning cup of coffee and another pill to take. They stood there and watched me drink my coffee.

"I handmade you a chicken casserole last night and put it in your refrigerator," he said.

"That's so sweet. Let me get up, and I'll warm us up a plate. I won't be able to eat it all."

"Thanks, but we ate just a few hours ago. You go ahead. Let's get you feeling better. You stay in bed, and I'll bring it to you."

He went in the kitchen, and few minutes later, I heard the microwave going off. He brought me my plate and motioned for me to eat some. I tried. I could only eat a couple of bites because my stomach had shrunk. I had already dropped several sizes and was steadily losing more weight. I had tried for years to lose weight. I was planning to join a gym and make time for exercising.

The next week I was lying in bed when the phone rang. It was seven o'clock Sunday morning. I thought, *Who*

in the devil is that? I was shocked to find that it was FEMA on the other end.

The lady on the line said, "You are being deployed tomorrow to do some adjuster work. There's been a flash flood somewhere in the world, and FEMA needs your help."

"I can. Where will I be going?"

She said, "Ma'am, I really don't know. You will know when you pick up your ticket at the Pensacola airport in the morning. I'm sorry I don't know more."

"Man, you guys are like spies. How should I pack if I don't know where I'm going?"

She laughed. "You are too funny. Pack for anything hot or cold, and you should be fine."

I called Gregory to tell him the great news. Some people sign up for FEMA and never get that call. Others sign up and it may take ten years for the phone to ring. It only took me two months before my number came up.

"Wynona, you can't go anywhere as sick as you are," he said.

"I don't care. This is a chance of a lifetime, and I want the experience." I had made up my mind. I was going. I just needed Gregory and Joshua to give me a ride the next day to the airport.

The next morning I awoke to a beautiful day. I was all excited about the adventure I was about to undertake. I had no idea where I was going, but I knew one thing: I would not know anybody there. I had just finished getting ready when Gregory and Joshua walked into the purple house. Gregory came over to me and gave me my normal morning coffee then loaded the luggage in the back of the Jeep. We all got in the Jeep and made the short, thirty-minute ride to the Pensacola Airport. On the way, they hardly spoke a word. I almost asked what was wrong but was just too excited to give a damn. We stopped curbside, and Gregory unloaded my luggage. He rolled it inside to the check-in desk. I waited my time in line, hoping I could make it before I had to vomit or faint. I started feeling bad and began to sweat. I needed to sit down and rest, but there was not enough time. I made it to the check-in counter and got my ticket. The woman at the counter checked in my luggage and told me to have a nice flight.

As we walked away, I opened my ticket to see my destination. It was Milwaukee, Wisconsin. *Ugh! Oh well, how bad could Milwaukee be?* At least I had never been there. Hopefully, it would be a good experience. I just hated cold weather. Gregory, Joshua, and I went upstairs to the bar. We all decided to have a cocktail since it would be two hours before I could get on the plane. We sat there and talked for an hour.

"I better get headed back to the office and get some work done. You better get headed to your gate so you don't have to rush in case you have to rest a lot. You are still very weak," Gregory said. I agreed, and we all took off in different directions. I started walking to the terminal and got halfway there. I became lightheaded and decided to sit down for a few minutes. I sat there longer than I thought when all of a sudden I heard them call my flight. It was time to board the airplane. I knew I had to give it what little gas I had in me to get there. I was the last one to board. I found my seat and settled in for the flight.

The flight finally took off, and I soon fell fast asleep. When I woke up, we were landing in Milwaukee. After I left the baggage claim area, I walked to the rental car agency to rent a car. I was wondering if that was a good idea. I had not driven in over two months. I decided I had to just suck it up and get it done. So I prayed that I would not fall asleep behind the wheel while cruising down the road to see clients. I picked up my rental car and headed to the hotel across the street.

I found the hotel and checked in. I asked for a wake-up call then went to my room to settle in. I ordered room service and passed out watching the evening news. The ringing phone woke me from my coma the next morning. I ordered a pot of coffee for breakfast then made my way downstairs to make the FEMA training session I was required to attend.

When I got to the meeting room, it was full of unfamiliar faces. I got my FEMA badge and found a seat in the middle of the room.

Before the meeting started, a lady tapped me on the shoulder. "May I sit next you?"

"Sure, chick. My name is Wynona," I said.

She sat down. "I'm Kelly from Tennessee," she said.

We talked during breaks and even had lunch together. After a long day of training, it was time to pick up our computers to see how many claims we had. Kelly and I went back to my room. She plugged up both computers and turned them on. She had five to do the next day, and I had fifteen. FEMA got that backward, on par with the rest of the federal government. She had all the experience, and I had none except for the one day of training. We turned off the computers and decided to go downstairs for dinner. We sat at the bar and met a few more adjusters. Everyone talked about how much money they were going to make. I was just there for the experience, and if I made good money, that would be icing on the cake. Everyone retired to their rooms to get a good night's sleep and an early start the next day.

I slept well that night but was not feeling so great the next day. I decided to take the day off and rest. I figured I would work twice as hard the next day to catch up. I lay around the room, resting and watching TV. In the afternoon, I decided to turn my computer on to get familiar with it. I figured out a few things, but not enough to go see a client. I had decided I had enough of the computer when the cell phone rang. It was Kelly. She was back at the hotel and wanted to know if I wanted to go to dinner.

We met and ordered.

"How did your day go?" I asked.

"Pretty good. I managed to get all five claims done. Lucky for me they were all right here around the hotel. I don't think any of them was more than five miles away. I have to finish up my paperwork and download the files to the home office. So I can't stay too long. How did you make out?"

"I stayed at the hotel and did nothing all day."

She started laughing. "If the head adjuster finds out, you're gonna be in trouble."

"No worries."

"You need to go back to your room and call your client list," she said.

I called all fifteen people and only had two answers to make appointments. One was at eleven and the other at three. I asked for directions and found out that my appointments were all the way across town in the hood.

I was awake before the phone rang and was headed down to breakfast full of energy. Well, maybe not full, but with more than I'd had in months. I was surprised breakfast was staying down as I sped down the interstate looking for my exit. In no time I was at my first appointment of the day.

As I was walking up to the front door, I stopped and looked around. I was in what seemed a nice black neighborhood. I knocked on the front door and the owner answered. She was a black woman, about five feet tall, and in her late sixties.

"Please, come in," she said.

We went to the kitchen and sat down at the table.

"Ma'am, do you have any damages to your basement?"

"Yes, ma'am, I sure do." She beamed.

"Would you take me down there so you can show me the damage?"

She led me down a tight stairway to the basement. When we got to the basement, I looked around. It was packed full of clothes and boxes. There was a washer and dryer in the back corner. *Odd*, I thought, *there are no unusual odors.*

"How high did the water get?"

"'Bout a foot."

I looked on the concrete block wall and saw no water line.

"Do you have a sump pump?"

"Uh-huh."

Undaunted by what I saw, I asked, "Is it working still?"

"Yes, it works just fine."

"What was damaged?"

She said, "My washer and dryer."

"And all of this stuff was here during the flood?"

"Oh yes, it was all down here."

The boxes were stacked on the floor and dry. There was no evidence they had ever gotten wet.

"That's fine. I'll put that in my report." I concluded my visit and headed back to the rental car.

Since my next appointment was three hours away, I decided to get some lunch. I headed toward my next appointment looking for a place to chow. A couple of miles down the road, I found a fast-food chicken place. I went inside, ordered, and sat down to eat. I felt like people were staring at me. They were. When I looked around, I discovered I was the minority. I flipped my long, dark-brown hair so they could see my FEMA badge clipped at the top of my shirt. Then everything was fine. I was the money chick. I got back in my car and headed for my last appointment.

I rode around for hours looking for the next lady's house and could never find it. I called her from my cell phone, and she never answered so I cruised back to the hotel. I dropped everything off at my room and headed to the lounge for supper. Kelly was already there. She had just picked up her cell phone to call me when I walked in and took a seat right beside her.

"So, how did you make out on day two?" she asked.

"It sucked. The one appointment I had was a disaster. All that training FEMA provided me did not apply in the real world."

"After we eat, I'll go back to your room and see if I can help you a bit."

I thought that was real kind since she had her own work to finish. When she got to my room, she turned on my computer and pulled up the one claim I had done. Shortly thereafter she started shaking her head. I found out I hadn't gotten things just right, and she quickly made the corrections. Then she showed me what she had done. "Have you checked in with your team leader?"

"Who would that be?" I asked.

"Every day, after you're finished with an appointment, you are supposed to check in. I'll go downstairs and get his name and number for you," she said.

When I called, the head adjuster asked, "Why haven't you been checking in with me?"

"Nobody bothered to tell me I needed to."

"I had about decided that you were missing. I was just about to send the search crew for you. Glad to know you're okay. Don't forget to check in after each appointment, okay," he said.

I fell into my bed after we got off the phone, exhausted. I lay there just thinking about my appointments and what they might go like when I conked out.

I woke up feeling even better than the day before, so I dressed and went downstairs. I ate, and it was time to get to my first appointment. I had three appointments that day and was ready to get started. My first appointment was with a lady thirty minutes away. She was a sweet elderly black lady. When I knocked on her front door, she answered and invited me inside.

"Ma'am, did you have any damages caused by the flood?"

"I had a lot of water down in my basement."

Down to the basement we went. I turned around to look at the damage the water had done to the carpet on her stairs.

"How high did the water get?"

"Right there to the top of the second step," she said, pointing.

"And how long did the water stay? Was it over night or longer?"

"I called the same day it happened, but nobody came. I recon about a little more than a day."

"Why do you suppose the carpet that got flooded looks as good as rest of it?" I asked, skeptical.

"Well, that's 'cause I did me a real good job cleaning it with Clorox," she insisted.

"Yes, ma'am. I'll put that in my report. Why do you suppose the wood isn't damaged on your bar?" I managed to ask without laughing.

"Oh, that's 'cause I got me some of that special wood."

I choked back my laughter again. "You know, where I'm from, we have hurricanes, and every one there would love to have some of that special wood."

I turned around to see what was behind me. I spotted a big screen TV. "Was it down here in the flood? Does it still work?"

"Yes, it was down here then. I saved it because I unplugged it."

"Yes, ma'am. I will put that in my report." I tried not to crack up.

We went back upstairs for her to sign the necessary paperwork. I thanked her for her time and told her FEMA would send her a letter in the next two weeks to let her know if she had been approved. She thanked me for my troubles, and out the door I went. I could not wait to get in the car. I had been holding back the laughter because of that "special wood." Once I shut the door, I started laughing and could not stop. Riding down the road laughing by yourself kind of makes you look crazy. I could not help it. I had heard some stories in my time, but that one took the cake.

I called my next appointment to get directions from where I was at. There was no answer so I left a message. I headed to my team leader's hotel. He pulled my claims up and was shocked. It was all wrong.

"Look, it's not my fault. When FEMA called to deploy me, they said the first three days I would have someone riding with me to train me. That didn't happen."

"I'll help you fix these. Tomorrow I'll ride with you and get you straightened out. Call me in the morning, and let me know when your first appointment is, and we'll meet then," he said.

"That would be awesome! Talk to you in the morning." On the way back to my room, my cell phone rang. It was Kelly. She was already at the lounge waiting on me to get back so we could order dinner. I was already on the interstate and made it back in fifteen minutes.

I met Kelly at the bar for dinner. I was still tired and still was not well from the spider bites. Even though I had been there several days, the purple spots on my arms kept popping up. I could not understand that. I called Gregory to check in.

"How's the big adventure going? Are you feeling any better?"

"Tons better. I've been able to eat and keep down three meals a day. The big adventure has had its moments. I'm ready to head back south," I admitted.

"I bet you're feeling better because they don't have spiders in Wisconsin. I've got things under control here, but Joshua and I miss you. Hurry home."

With that, we said our good-byes, and I continued my dinner with Kelly. Kelly decided that she would check out of her room and take the spare bed in my room. I figured that may not be a bad idea. I could use her help and didn't mind her company. She paid me cash for her share, and I scribbled a handwritten receipt so she could take it as a tax deduction.

I woke up the next day healthy and happy. I was ready to get my day started. I ate breakfast at the hotel and headed for the car. I called my team leader as I pulled out of the parking lot to let him know I was on my way. When I arrived at my first appointment, he was already there sitting in his car. He saw me pull up to the curb, and we both got out. We walked to the door and knocked. The lady of the house opened the door and let us in. I watched as he asked her questions and did the claim. He only took fifteen minutes for him to complete. We walked back to our cars, and he said he would see me later at his hotel. It was nice of him to help, but I learned nothing. I went to my next appointment alone.

I had been there for eight days and was getting tired of the big city. I was ready to go back to Orange Beach. When I got back to the hotel, there was a message on my room phone. It was from headquarters saying they needed to talk to me. I immediately went downstairs. My boss was sitting there.

"You have really been doing a good job, but they had to let some of the adjusters go home. FEMA hired too many of us for the damage that had been done. I wanted to give you a choice of staying or heading back home," he said.

That was a Godsend. I had my fill of this adventure and was ready for it to end. He wrote down an eight hundred number to call to make the flight arrangements. I almost ran to the nearest phone when I remembered cell phones existed. I was homesick and ready to see my Little Dude.

Once the arrangements were made, I called Little Dude. I wanted him to know I would be home in two days. I could hear the excitement in his voice. Next I called Gregory to let him know my flight arrangements so he and Joshua could pick me up. The next day I did nothing but wash clothes and pack. I went to the bar late that day to say bye to my new friends, especially Kelly. Everyone wished me well. I got a good night's sleep and woke up the next day ready to go.

I gathered my suitcases and went down to the front desk to check out. I paid my hotel bill and went to the airport to turn in the rental car. I caught my flight on time and we landed in Pensacola safely. I even stayed awake most of the flight back. Gregory and Joshua were there waiting for me with a present. I looked into the bag, and it was a bottle of some expensive perfume. I hugged their necks and thanked them. We got my luggage and stopped at a restaurant for dinner and wine. We left, and they took me home. Was it ever nice to see my purple house on the bluff.

The next day was back to normal. Gregory and Joshua came by to feed the dogs and bring me a cup of coffee. After I was home for several days, back to bed I went.

"Looks like those spiders are at it again. You really gotta find a way to get rid of them," Gregory said. This time I was sicker than before the trip. Both my arms were covered in purple spots. I even found some on my legs this time. I did not feel like seeing anybody, not even Gregory and Joshua. I turned my cell phone off and just lay in bed and slept.

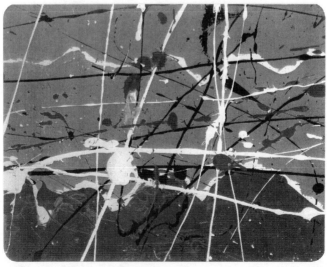

David
2002

bivdo

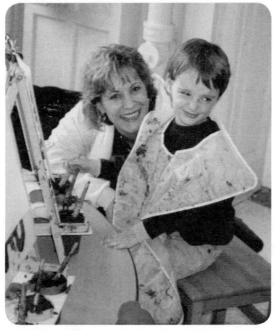

THE COMPLAINT

I stayed sick for three more months. I would try to make it to the office every day.

Gregory would always tell me, "You don't look good at all, Wynona. Why don't you go home and try and get some rest."

I was too stubborn and had stopped taking his advice. Besides, I had a business to run. I'd come in and usually stayed till lunch. One day I toughed it out and stayed till four. I'm five foot ten. I had gotten down to just over a hundred pounds, a shadow of what I was just a few months earlier. I was so sick that all I wanted was water—no coffee, no food, no anything.

Gregory kept bringing me a cup of coffee every morning. I would sit on the porch and act like I was drinking it. After they would leave, I would go inside and pour it down the drain. I started feeling better. I got well enough to start coming in a few more hours a day. A week went by, and I was feeling pretty good. I was at the job I loved, and business was good. I asked Gregory for the last three months' bank statements and the last three credit card statements so I could see what kind of a budget I was on. He said he was really busy and would give them to me later. I got busy selling insurance and forgot about it.

We were so busy at work, I decided to hire another person. My cousin's husband, Oscar, was recently out of work and needed a job. He had accounting experience so I decided to bring him in to help keep up with my accounting since Gregory was swamped. I did not discuss it with Gregory because I figured he would try and talk me out of it. I called Oscar and told him to be at work on Monday.

When Oscar walked in, Gregory asked him, "May I help you?"

"No thanks. I'm Wynona's cousin-in-law, Oscar. I'm just here to help her catch up on some accounting work," he said.

I moved Joshua out of his office and gave it to Oscar. He needed a desk and a computer to work on. All at once Gregory was in a really bad mood. It was like someone had just stepped on his manhood. Gregory just stomped back to his office and didn't say another word to anybody. I thought he was offended because I had thrown Joshua out of his office. The next couple of weeks were uncomfortable.

Oscar had been working for me for about a month when I got a call. It was the head investigator for the Alabama Insurance Department. Her name was Beau. She had received a complaint from a client I had insured a mobile home for in Elberta, Alabama. She wanted to make an appointment to come see me. We set up our meeting for Friday at ten. She wanted his file and the last two months of the company bank statements. I got off the phone and went to Gregory's office.

"The insurance investigator will be here on Friday. How 'bout make some magic happen and get me my bank statements for the last two months and pull some guy named J.G. Klein's file."

He quickly closed whatever he was doing on his computer and leaned forward on his desk.

"What do they want?"

"I don't know, dude. Something about a wind policy. Just get them together, okay. I don't feel good, and I'm not in the mood to ask for things twice, okay?"

I don't know if I pissed him off or what, but he sank back in his chair contemplating something as he chewed the end of his pen.

"Sure, Wynona. I'll have them for you by Friday. Let me get back to what I was doing. I'm kind of busy."

He seemed more interested in what he was doing than listening to me and basically put me on hold. If I had more energy, I would have read him the Riot Act. The phones were ringing, and I took a few sales calls then headed home.

Friday was already here. I tightened up some loose ends and got ready for Beau to arrive.

"Oh, Gregory, where are my files, *dear*?" I asked.

"Um… I'll have to find them. Hold on."

"You have got to be kidding me, dude! I asked you to get that stuff together days ago. She's going to be here any second. Don't make me stuff my foot where it's not supposed to be. Get me my files, el-pronto! *Comprendo?*"

He stormed out of my office and returned with the file.

"And how about the bank statements?" I threw my arms open. "Today, Gregory, today."

He threw the file onto my desk and got all pissy.

"I'm working on it. Damn!" he said and disappeared again.

Moments later, Beau showed up with a retired FBI agent named Don. They came in, shook my hand, and sat down. Immediately she got down to business.

"I received a call from a man in Elberta. He stated that he bought a mobile home policy excluding wind. After he took out the policy, he decided to take out a separate wind policy. He met with Gregory to do the paperwork and pay the premium," Beau explained.

"Gregory, please come to my office," I said, holding the intercom button down.

"What can I do for you, *Wynona*," he said, his voice dripping in extreme sarcasm.

"Well, you can start with dropping the attitude and tell this lady here what you know about the file on Mr. Klein. He says you met with him."

He glanced at the file and quickly handed it back to me.

"I don't remember him at all, Wynona."

"I really don't remember," he said.

Beau rolled her eyes at Gregory's answer. She opened the file and removed some paperwork and handed it to me.

"Would you mind making me copies of these?" She handed me the deck page that showed the coverage that was in force. It showed just basic coverage and excluded wind. It was just the way I remembered. I gave her the copies and didn't really expect to hear from her again.

"It's not a problem except that the man from Elberta called the state wind pool to see how much his renewal premium would be. The wind pool told him they had never heard of him. That's why he called the Alabama Insurance Department and made the complaint with us. I'll do some more investigating and be in touch."

Gregory left his perch at the door to my office.

"No worries. We'll be here. Stop by anytime."

And with that, she got up, shook my hand, and quietly walked out of my office. I followed them out of my office and to the lobby where I found Gregory, all ready upset over Oscar's presence, walking around like he was barefoot on a asphalt road in the hot July sun.

I still wanted my bank statements so I could verify that I was giving Beau accurate information.

"Look, dude, they're gone now. If I don't have those bank statements in my little hand—"

The phone rang, and I remembered I was expecting a call from an important client.

"I'm taking the rest of the afternoon off. You just don't know when to quit bugging me. I said I'll get to it, and I will. Just get off my back!" He left just as my client began to speak.

It was a long call. I was still irritated at Gregory when I finished with the client and decided to do something to get his attention. I wasn't worried about the investigator, but Gregory sure had pissed me off. I decided that if that's the way it was, I'd punish him by taking all the incoming calls myself. I went to their desks and confiscated the telephones. *Now maybe he won't be to busy to get me my frigging files.* I laughed to myself as I locked the front door and headed home.

I made sure I got to work before the guys Monday morning. Freaked out doesn't do justice to the look on Gregory's face.

"Where the hell are the phones, Wynona?"

"In a safe place, dude! The only thing you need to be working on right now is getting me those bank statements. Until I get them, you don't get the phone back. Got me?"

After two hours of answering the phone, it was actually getting to be more than I could handle. I made Gregory promise to get me my statements and gave them their phones back. The day flew by. I was still waiting for the statements when four o'clock rolled around. He walked over to me and gave me a peck on the cheek. Gregory and Joshua headed out the door as I talked to Oscar and Babe about their tasks. I was totally disgusted that he Gregory left again with out giving the statements to me. I looked at the clock and realized I was running late for Little Dude's practice.

"Can you pull up QuickBooks and print the statements for me, Oscar."

"Sure, coz. What's the password?"

I divulged the secret password and gathered up my keys and headed to the door.

"I have to take Little Dude to football practice in Orange Beach. I'll be right back."

On the short trip to practice, I thought it was good that Gregory hadn't changed the password. Now I could get my closure to the situation with the man from Elberta. I decided that when I saw him, I'd have a heart-to-heart with him about who the boss was and try and find out why he couldn't deal with Oscar helping us in the office.

When I got back to the office after dropping Little Dude off at practice, I got another unwanted surprise. Oscar was sitting at Gregory's desk; Babe stood beside him.

"You better sit down. You aren't going to like what I have to show you," he said.

Oscar gave me the printout of quick books to look at. He was right—I did need to sit down. Gregory had paid himself year to date $273,000. To say I was devastated would be a major understatement. *How could this have happened?* Gregory was like a brother to me and also a Baptist missionary. He loved me like a sister. I was his best man/chick when he had married Joshua a few months earlier while in California. We were tight and watched each other's back. I thought that was bad enough.

I was dumbfounded. "Thanks for showing me. Any chance you would be willing to come in early in the morning? I'm gonna have it out with that SOB! I may need you to back me up."

"You know you can't do that. They will throw you in jail. I'll be here with you early tomorrow. You can count on me, coz," he said.

I felt like a fish. He had already set the hook, reeled me in, and filleted me, and I didn't even see the bait. My anger boiled like the oil in a frying pan. I was smoking hot and bursting into flames. I tried to get some rest; it was no use. It was like I was stuck in the *Twilight Zone*. Nothing seemed real.

The next morning I got to work and anxiously waited Gregory's arrival. I sat there thirty minutes. Gregory and Joshua never showed up. The gig was up, and Gregory knew it. Oscar arrived, and we went inside to see if we could find out what the damages were. I called the bank to order copies of the last three monthly statements. I requested copies of the checks both front and back that he had deposited and had written. The branch manager let me know I would have them in a couple of days. When I hung up the phone, it immediately rang. It was Beau.

"I need to come see you and Gregory in the morning," she said.

"Gregory no longer works here."

"That's a good thing. What time is good for you?"

"Ma'am, you can come at whatever time you want to show up. Looks like I'm gonna be rather busy so I'll be here all the time," I answered.

I went on to work the rest of the day as best I could. That was on a Wednesday.

Beau showed up the next day around nine. She came in and sat at the front of my desk. She had a copy of the check that the man from Elberta had written to Starfish.

"It was deposited at Vision Bank in Elberta. Gregory also has a checking account there. All the tellers said they knew him because he came in a lot," Beau said.

"I will make it good," I said.

That was the first fraud case. I prayed it was the only one, but my gut told me otherwise.

"You need to run an AD in the local paper. There maybe other fraud cases. I'll be back in touch."

"How long do I have to run them? What does it have to say?"

"It need's to run for sixty days. It should read something like, 'If you think you have insurance with Starfish, call' then your number, etc. The quicker you do this, the better."

"Don't worry, ma'am. I'll place the AD when we're done here."

"We're done for now. Good-bye."

I didn't like the way she said the "for now" part. I knew I was screwed. With Gregory on the run, all I could do was do damage control and move forward. I felt physically ill. His betrayal made me feel worse than the spider bites ever did.

The day the AD came out, the office phone and cell phone started ringing off the hook. It was the middle of summer and hurricane season. Most of my clients had sunk their life savings into their homes and were nervous. I made so many appointments, by the end of the day I filled the next two weeks.

The first clients I saw were a couple that lived in Gulf Shores. The lady handed me her declaration page. She wanted to know if her policy was any good. I called the underwriter to see. The declaration page she showed me looked like none I had ever seen. It looked real, all right. It had a policy number, effective and expiration date, the coverage amounts, and their name and address. What was different was that the print was tiny. It was on yellow paper instead of the white they normally came on. I picked up the phone and called my underwriter, Todd I explained the situation to him and gave him the policy number. Sure enough, it was a fake.

"Do you want a refund, or would you like a new policy?"

"Our life's savings is tied up in our house. We have to have it covered," the gentleman replied.

Naturally, I wrote them a new policy and paid their premium from my company account. I promised them that as soon as Todd sent me their policy, I would forward it to them or they could come by and pick it up in person, either was fine with me. They thanked me, and out the door they went.

Next was my real good friend Sunny. We had met a couple of years earlier when he helped build my purple house. We had been great friends ever since. He sat down and asked me to check both his policies. I did, and they were fraud. He already knew it wasn't me that took his money.

He looked at me and said, "That pisses me off, Winnie. I am ready for the redneck in me to come out if he ever shows back up. Just write me some new polices, and I'm good."

So I did.

"I noticed coming in that your grass needs cutting and bushes need to be trimmed. Would you mind if I did them for you?" he asked.

"Thanks, dude. But currently I can't afford any extras until I know how much Gregory has taken."

He just grinned. "Winnie, you know I love you. I will be back tomorrow and do it for nothing."

People around here are like that. They see someone suffering and they try to lend a hand, even if it's something small like that. It really made my day.

My receptionist quit, for no apparent reason, and with everything in such chaos, mom volunteered to be my receptionist. Everybody that came by just loved her. When Sunny left, Mom stepped into my office. "There are ten people in the lobby to see you."

"Okay, Mama, you can send the next one back."

The next client was a younger guy who lived two blocks from the beach in Gulf Shores. He also had a policy that was a fraud. He opted for a refund. As I told him when he could come by and pick up his check, he looked at me and smiled. I found no humor in what had happened to me so I was ready to see his backside.

"Did you know about the embezzlement that happened when Gregory and Evan worked at a soda bottling plant several years ago?" he asked.

"No. Tell me," I said. I decided he could stay at least another minute. I wondered if he noticed my chin sitting on the floor.

"Gregory and Evan worked at the soda factory for a year before it came to light. Gregory had learned well from his father, Evan. As it was told to me, they both embezzled money from the soda factory. When they were caught, Evan took the fall and went to prison. Gregory claimed he was innocent, and no charges were brought against him. He still had a clean record even though he was guilty."

"Evan too? I'd love to hear more, but I have to get some lunch. Come by sometime if you hear more."

"No problem. I will. Take care," he said.

They say that the apple doesn't fall far from the tree. If Gregory is the bad apple, then that makes Evan "Johnny Bad-Appleseed."

What a revelation. I let Little Dude stay with a convicted felon for a week. *Could Gregory's whole family be in on this?* I wondered. I didn't think I could get more stressed, but I did.

He left, and I waited for the next person.

Next was a lady who lived down Ft. Morgan Road. She came in laughing. I wondered what she found to be so funny. It was nice to see a smiling face.

She took a seat. "Did you know that my husband was a commercial airline pilot?" she asked.

I admitted I didn't.

"He called me last night from Nashville, Tennessee. He was in his hotel room watching the six o'clock news when your picture appeared on TV, and they reported what was happening to your company."

I had made the local newspaper the week before, and now the networks were running the story too. He sent his wife to see me to see if they had insurance.

"I know we do because when we took out the policy, we overpaid. We got a refund check in the mail for one hundred and thirty dollars from the insurance company."

I called Todd just to make sure. Luckily, she was correct. Their policy was legit.

"You are correct. Your policy is in order. Thanks for your loyalty."

"Thank you. We'll see you next year when we renew again," she said.

About that time the phone rang. It was a missionary named Joseph. He had been in Turkey doing God's work and had just landed in the USA.

"I was a missionary in Turkey in 2004 with Gregory. We both worked for the International Baptist Mission Board. Gregory was caught stealing over five hundred thousand dollars from Lotti Moon and the Earthquake Relief Fund. When the International Baptist Mission Board caught him, all they did was fire him and make him sign a note promising to repay the money he took. He made one payment of ten thousand dollars then went on the run. They put a judgment on his credit but never had him charged with the crime. Gregory got caught when the IBM approved to install an elevator at a local apartment complex. There was a man that owned a unit there and could not walk up and down the stairs. When he went to stay at his condo, to his disappointment, there was no elevator. He turned it in to the IBM to investigate. I went to the board and asked for an external audit. The board of directors said they would. If they did, I never saw it. Instead the IBM fired me for speaking out. If you are a non-profit organization, you are supposed to have an audit done once a year. Then it's made available to the public. That was not the case. Now I'm an independent missionary. I'm on my way home to Louisiana to raise money to purchase Bibles for my ministry. I was wondering if I could stop by and speak with you sometime next week," Joseph said.

I was nearly speechless. "Sure. I'm here Monday to Friday, eight to four."

My head was spinning. With my heart racing out of control, I left the office to get some fresh air. When I came back in, I had one after another show up to check their insurance. It ended up that two out of three were fraud. Sitting at my desk, I wondered just how many clients had been fraud cases. *How much money did I owe?*

Before I left that day, I decided to check on my homeowners and rental house insurance. I just knew mine were good. I had written my own policies, bound the coverage, and paid the premiums. When I called

Todd, he looked me up and let me know they were no good.

"You bound the policies, but the premium payment never got to us, Wynona. As you know that means they automatically got canceled."

Gregory had even told me one day that my homeowner's policy had come in the mail and he had stuck it in my file. My fury grew every second, and it was all I could to keep myself from doing something stupid. I trusted him so much; I never checked. That was my fault. I fell deeper into the bottomless pit I found myself in.

I went out front to talk to Mom.

"I'm ruined, Mama. I'm out of cash. The bank told me they were done paying for fraud and they were starting with me. I guess the insurance you get from the FDIC isn't worth the paper it's printed on." I couldn't hold the tears back any longer. Mom gave me a hug; I sobbed uncontrollably.

"There, there, dear. Bad things happen to good people. Don't you worry your sweet little head

anymore. I've still got an annuity I can cash in to help. You know you mean the world to me."

It felt good to be held by her.

"I'll pay you back as soon as I can, Mama," I muttered out between sobs.

She just smiled. "Don't worry, doll. I don't care if you don't ever pay it back."

I felt true comfort as we embraced.

I thanked God for giving me such an awesome mom.

Knights in Cheap Clothing

The day after Gregory left, I went to the Gulf Shores Police Department to file a theft report. Officer Sock took the report.

Two weeks after Gregory left, I went to work to see what the day had in store for me. I got to work and had to park next door. There was a yellow tape tied to my sign. It stretched to the end of the parking lot where it wrapped around a trashcan then crossed the parking lot to another trashcan then went back to the fence alongside the building. All it said was "Caution. Do not cross." It looked like a crime scene. About the time I got out of the truck, Oscar pulled up.

He got out of his car he pointed at the tape and asked me, "What is that all about?"

"Dude, I have no idea. But I'm gonna find out pretty quick."

I called Judge Buck.

"Don't go inside until I can get Sock over there to investigate. We'll get to the bottom of it, Wynona," he said.

It took officer Sock over an hour to make the mile ride from the station to my office. Oscar and I brainstormed. We couldn't figure out who could have put up the tape. Was it the insurance commissioner, one of the feds? Maybe it was Gregory. Was I shut down? All it did was stress me out to say the least. When Officer Sock pulled into the parking lot, he slowly got out of his police car. He walked over to the tape and just started shaking his head.

I walked up to him and asked him, "Who do you think put this up?"

"Wyoma,"—he could not pronounce *Wynona*—"someone is playing a cruel joke on you. I know it wasn't any law enforcement agency. If had been they would have notified me, and no one has called the department. Besides that, it's not the tape we use. That tape is from a hardware store. The stuff they use in construction. If it was official it would say 'Crime Scene. Do Not Cross.'"

He gathered up the tape to take it to the police department to see if he could get any fingerprints off it. Nothing ever showed up. Officer Sock left, and Oscar and I went inside to go to work. I was so busy straightening out the mess Gregory had made that I had to stay late to catch up on normal business matters. Total exhaustion set in, and I grew more depressed.

Later that day my friend Jim came in to see me. I told him about the tape in the parking lot. He let me know he stopped by because he sold Gregory and Joshua a house and owner financed them. Someone had come in the middle of the night and stole all the door knobs, appliances, the central heating unit, and every light bulb in the place.

"I should have known something was up when they gave me a brown paper bag with fifty grand in it when they paid the down payment." He seemed embarrassed for not telling me before.

"You think? Only people with something to hide lay out that kind of money in cash."

"No. You're right. I should have known better. I guess I'll just have to file a theft claim to make it all right."

"Well, you can file one, but they are going to turn you down. I'll have to let the adjuster know that the house had been sold and was vacant at the time of the theft." I was fuming.

"Then I guess we both got screwed," he said, and in a huff and a puff, he was gone.

He had just irritated the crap out of me. I wanted to go after him and tell him what a jerk he was to show up and even suggest such. He took fifty grand of my money and came to cry to me when he got taken. Maybe he ought to give me my money back. The nerve! Instead, I let it go and decided to go home early.

Oscars lack of driving skills led to him wrecking his father-in-law's truck two days in one week and got his ride pulled. I was in the market for a new book-keeper—again. A client of mine named Lou called one day about her insurance. During that call she said she knew I needed some help. She reminded that bookkeeping had been her occupation for all the years I knew her. She offered to come work for me starting the next day. I gladly hired her and put her to work as soon as she arrived.

Mom showed up the next day with a check. I put the six-figure check in my operating account thinking that would be enough. As it ended up, that was nothing more than a drop in the bucket. When I got back from the bank, I had a lobby full of people waiting on me. I was feeling the bad day coming at me already. Feeling near defeat, I dug down deep for the courage to make it through the day. I had to make it through this for Little Dude.

The first couple was a retired couple from Daphne. They had purchased a homeowner's policy from Gregory while I was out sick with spider bites. I had never met them before or even heard of them. He showed me his declaration page; it was a fake.

"Would y'all like a new policy or a refund?"

"We know it's not your fault. We've been following what happened in the paper. We'll just take another policy," he said.

As I wrote their new policy, he continued, "I used to be a prison guard at a state prison. I've seen a lot of things doing that kind of work. Have you ever heard of 'face down?'"

"I have no idea, sir."

"It's what's goin' to happen when they catch Gregory and he gets to prison." He began to describe what it really meant, but I stopped him in midsentence.

"Personally, I don't care what happens to him. He'll deserve what ever happens, but I don't care to hear that kind of thing. Thank y'all for your concern. I'm sorry you got to be his victims, too."

I finished the paperwork and paid their premium. Although the premium was more than they originally paid, I covered the whole amount. They thanked me and left.

The next client walked in and presented his policy for me to check. My heart sunk as I saw the familiar yellow paper. I knew it was fake. This time I did not call Todd. I just got up and got his file from the filing cabinet. I walked back in my office, sat down, and opened up the file. I looked up at him and told him it was fake.

"I've known you for years, Wynona, and I know you are honest and will do the right thing."

As I was writing his new policy, he asked, "Is the secret service involved in the investigation?"

"As far as I know, it's just the insurance commissioner and the Gulf Shores Police. I did call the FBI. They asked me for my agent's name, but I didn't have one. She was rude. She said not to call back till I have a name. So I gave up. If they wouldn't give me one, how am I supposed to get one?"

"I used to be the chief of police in Gulf Shores. This is more than they can handle. I'm going to do you a favor and call my brother. He's an agent for the CIA. If anyone can help you it's him."

He began making the call as I sat there hoping he was right. If anyone needed some help right now, it was me. When he got off the phone, he looked at me and smiled.

"He'll call you before five and have you an agent's name."

I shook his hand as he stood to leave.

Humble and moved by his help, I told him, "Dude, you have no idea how much I appreciate what you just did. Thank you."

There were a dozen more people that stopped in to check their policies, and the day zipped by. It was 4:57 p.m. when the phone rang; it was him.

My heart raced. "I have a number and a name for you. The secret service agent is sitting by his phone waiting for your call. Good luck."

"Yes, sir. I'll call him right now. Thank you so much."

I took a deep breath and I dialed the number he gave me. It rang three times before someone answered.

"May I speak with Agent Kellie?"

"May I ask who's calling, ma'am?" came the voice on the other end.

"Yes, sir. This is Wynona. I'm calling about the insurance company I own."

They put me on hold then transferred me to Agent Kellie.

"Hi, Wynona. I got a call about you earlier. I was wondering if I could come see you some time next week."

"Yes, sir. The sooner the better."

"Okay then. I'll call you next Monday and set up the time. Talk to you then."

As he hung up the phone, I sighed and just sat there for a while. Monday was a long ways off. But at least it was something to look forward to for a change.

The next day I went to work as usual. I was walking into the office building, and my cell phone rang. It was Agent Kellie.

"Listen, I didn't realize the magnitude of what had happened. I have cleared my calendar, and I'd like to come by right now. If it's okay with you?"

My heart was filled with joy at his words.

"You bet. Come on," I said.

"We are in Mobile and will be there within the hour," he promised.

"Awesome! See you then."

An hour passed to the minute when two tall men walked into the front office. One asked Mom if they could see me. She got up and walked back to my office all nervous.

"The federal agents are here to see you."

"Well don't keep them waiting, Mama. Show them in."

I jumped out of my chair and met them halfway down the hallway to my office. I welcomed them to the disaster area and showed them to my office. They didn't look at all the way I had imagined them. There were no dark sunglasses. No earphone. Nothing. Until they showed me their badges, I wasn't totally convinced these guys weren't some of the local riffraff playing games with me. Agent Kellie was the one in shorts, a button-down Hawaiian shirt, and loafers. He apparently didn't hang out at the gym much. I swear he looked like an aged "Ace Ventura, Pet Detective." I swear he could have just come from hanging out with Jimmy Buffett at a bar, throwing back a few brews.

Agent Bob reminded me of all those James Bond movies. Only his suit looked like the ones you find at SK clothing stores marked three for one-hundred bucks. His cheap suit clashed with his four-hundred-dollar Italian wingtips. I wondered if the suit was one he had since he was a kid, high-water rising. If he was over thirty then I'm twenty-five. Something about his suit made me think of church. Neither looked like a fed. I guess that was the point.

They took a seat in front of my desk as they introduced themselves.

"We are only here to ask a few questions. It doesn't mean we will take your case," Agent Kellie said.

"I'm sure y'all will when you hear what I have to say," I said.

Agent Kellie started asking me some questions, and I answered as best I could. The two hours they were there flew by. Agent Kellie did all the talking while Agent Bob stared at me like he was trying to get into my head.

After they had all the information they asked for, Agent Kellie said, "We will definitely take your case!"

Finally: someone with connections who wanted to help me. A peace came over me, and I just knew Gregory was going to get caught and go to the jail. I'd get mine and my clients' money back, and then my fairytale life would be back. I began to think of the fun things Little Dude and I would do when this was over. The bonus would be that I would get to see him in court, wearing leg irons and handcuffs, sporting an orange jumpsuit that has "Property of Baldwin County" on the back. I smiled.

Agent Kellie requested the hard drive to Gregory's computer and the postal meter. I told them they could have everything in the office if it would help catch Gregory. Agent Kellie just laughed as he wrote me a receipt for the meter and Gregory's computer. I didn't care if I got either back, which was good because I didn't.

The next day I was pouring myself a cup of coffee and headed to my office when I heard a voice behind me say, "Hello, Wynona." I turned around to find a real estate friend of mine. I told him to come on back. He had built an apartment complex in Gulf Shores a couple of months earlier. He had gotten a quote while I was out sick. I never knew that he was a client until he showed up that day. He had taken out a commercial policy on the complex and had given Gregory a couple of checks. The following month is when it hit the paper about what Gregory had done, and he wanted to know if his policy was any good. I checked, and it was not. He did not have a copy of his policy, only of his two canceled checks.

As I looked at the first check. "How much was the down payment?"

"Five thousand for the down payment and then eleven hundred for the first monthly premium."

When I looked at one check he handed me, I saw that it had been altered.

"You need to call your bank. One has been altered to read fifteen thousand, and the other one here has been changed to eleven-thousand. You need to find out how much they actually paid."

Before I could finish what I was saying, he was dialing their number. When he got off the phone, he looked relived.

"She told me that the checks had cleared for the correct amount," he told me. Thank God. There was no apparent limit to the crimes Gregory would commit. He took out a new police and the down payment was only eighteen dollars more than he originally paid.

"I will take care of it," I said.

He thanked me and got out his checkbook and started writing.

"What are you doing?" I asked.

"I'm paying the difference, Wynona. I've known you over twenty years. I know you got ripped off. If I could afford it, I wouldn't let you pay anything. But at least let me pay the eighteen."

After he left, I could feel my emotions tormenting me. The rollercoaster kept racing down the hill, and my stomach was in my throat. I went home drained again and doomed to yet another restless night.

The next day I was between seeing clients when the phone rang. It was Beau from the Alabama Insurance Department. Hearing from her always made me sick to my stomach. She had finished her investigation and wanted to come see me. She suggested that I have my attorney present. My heart slid into my flip-flops. I did not understand why that was necessary since I was not guilty. Gregory was the one that stole all the money and forged the checks. She gave me a day and time. When I got off the phone with her, I called Judge Kevin. Amy, his receptionist, patched me through. I let him in on what Beau told me and set it up for him to contact them. He put me at the front of the line on his schedule.

The next morning, I got a visit from a customer who once told me he worked for the government. He came down from Huntsville to see me in person. He had thanked me for the work I did for him on his condo insurance. He let me know that he once guarded President Bush when he was with the secret service. If that was the case, then he already knew all about me, that they probably had my phones tapped and had been tailing me to see where I was going and who I was seeing. He confirmed my suspicions. I let him know I heard about "face down" but didn't really know what it meant.

"'Face down' means he's gonna be raped. It's not always with body parts, either," he said.

The days turned into weeks and the weeks into months. I began to wonder if my nightmare was ever going to end. Mom's annuity money ran out, and the fraud cases kept coming. I turned to Mom for advice. I had already cashed in all the life insurance policies I owned on me and Little Dude. All the money I was making was going straight back into the company to pay bills and fraud cases.

I had tried to make my mortgage payments on my purple house. It took me only three months after Gregory flew the coup like the chicken he was to realize I could not right the wrong he had done and pay my mortgage. I cried every day for two weeks knowing that I had finally made my dream come to true to see it slowly drift away. One day I woke up and decided I had enough. When they foreclosed, I would just peacefully go away.

Mom offered to talk to Baby Doll to see if she would buy out my interest in the penthouse condo. I was so distracted with everything, I hadn't even thought of it. *What choice did I have?* At the time I had no other options. The next day Mom came to work and said Baby Doll would be calling me with a closing date. Sure enough late that afternoon she called. The next week we were to close. Once it happened, the money went back into operating account to pay fraud cases. I just knew that was going to be the end of it.

I went to work the next day, and Pastor Roy came to see me. I had called him and told him I needed to write him some new insurance because his was no good. He walked into my office and gave me a big hug.

"You are the most-prayed for person I have ever met. If my policies are no good, just write me some new ones," he said.

So I did. He signed the paperwork and got out his checkbook. I argued that he couldn't pay for the policies, that I would take care of it. He resisted but ultimately gave in. Before he left, he let me know he'd be back to get his parents some insurance from me. He hugged my neck. I was so thankful he was the one who had baptized me.

The phone rang after Pastor Roy left. It was Dr. Martha. She wanted to know if her homeowner's was any good. I had her to hang on while I pulled her file and checked. I got back on the phone and let her know it was a fraud. I wanted to know what she wanted me to do. She remembered I had met with her while I was sick. It was one of the few days I had made it into the office. She knew about my troubles and knew I had done nothing wrong. She wanted me to see her at her office and write her a new policy. I told her I would be there in about thirty minutes. I got the paperwork I needed and went straight to her Foley office.

When I arrived I found her busy with a client. I sat down and waited for her to finish. It only took a few minutes for the client to leave and for her to tell me to come on over. I went and sat down in front of her desk to write her a new policy.

"How did you get that?" she asked, pointing to the baseball-size make on my elbow.

"I got bit by spiders several times. That's why I've been sick for the last six months. I've been on three different antibiotics trying to get over them."

She shook her head. "Wynona, that isn't from spiders, dear. You have been poisoned with arsenic. Once arsenic enters the bloodstream, it builds up in the joints. That's what the purple marks are from."

I nearly fainted at her words. Surely she was mistaken.

"Please tell me you're wrong. Besides, who could possibly want to kill little ole me?"

"I really wish I was wrong. I really wish I was."

I was so petrified and too upset to stay. I had to get some fresh air and quickly left her office.

I couldn't believe my ears. How could anyone be so cruel that they would try and murder me? I thanked her for the information and told her I would pay her first two payments. She would have to pay after that since that was all Gregory had stolen from her. As I cruised back to the office, I tried to figure out who it could be. Gregory never crossed my mind. I mean, I knew he was a thief, but a murderer, too? That was just too much for me to digest.

When I walked into the office, Mom and Lou were already there. Mom was at her desk trying to figure out how to open the revolver she was holding. I freaked out.

"Mama! What are you doing with that pistol?"

"I'm trying to load the damn thing. I'm not going to let Gregory get you. If he comes in here, I'll shoot him right in the eye!"

"Mama, he's not going to come back here. Now, I've got work to do so how 'bout put your six-shooter away. Let's not shoot anything, okay?"

She looked up at me and stuck out her bottom lip. I considered if I ought to take the bullets from her the way Andy would. As I walked past Lou's office, I motioned for her to follow me back to my office for a meeting.

"If you hear a gunshot, we're not getting robbed. It's Mama playing with her gun," I joked.

Lou started to ask me something on the way toward my office.

Ka-pow!

The shot rang in my eardrums.

"Oh my God!" Lou exclaimed. "Do you think she's okay?"

I ran around the corner to the receptionist desk. My eyes met Mom's. She looked at the trashcan under her desk then back at the smoking gun she held in her right hand.

"Mama, are you all right?"

"Yes. I'm fine. The trashcan isn't, though. I shot it. Oh, and the desk, too. I just wanted to make sure it worked before I gave it to you."

"All right, Annie Oakley, give me your gun. Your Wild West days are done. All right, everybody, back to what you were doing before wild woman here shot up the place. Let's get back to it. I had a smile on my face as I shook my head. Only my mom could do something like that. Whew!

That afternoon Pastor Roy stopped back by to see me. I told him what Dr. Martha had said. He was not surprised.

"I can tell you who did it," he said.

Wide-eyed, I asked, "Really? Who?"

"Gregory."

"How's that now?" I was dumbfounded.

"I figured out what Gregory planned to do. He was going to steal as much money as he could, and when it came to light what had happened, he was going to murder you. He would tell everyone that the shame was so great that you took your own life."

I sat there in shock. The bells were finally going off. I knew he was the devil on earth after all that I had been through. Pastor Roy took out some car insurance and told me he would see me Sunday.

"Ye-yes, sir, I will be there." I was in a complete daze as he left.

I picked up the phone and called Agent Kellie. He was at his office and answered my call.

"Hi, Agent Kellie. Thanks for taking my call. I just spoke with a doctor friend of mine, and she thinks my spider bites are sores from being poisoned. What should I do? He tried to kill me!"

"Hmm. I'm sorry, Wynona, in all the years I've been an agent, I've never had a living victim. By the time I see them, the forensics crew has already established how they died. I guess it would be best if you got a forensic hair test done right away."

"Who do I go to, to get one done? It's been over a year since I saw him, you know. Will the poison even show up?"

"If he used arsenic, it will still be there. I'm not really sure who you can get to do it. I wish I could be more helpful."

"It's okay, Agent Kellie. I'll figure that part out. When I get the results, I want him charged with attempted murder. I don't want him to see the outside for a very, very long time."

I decided to call Dr. Martha to see if she knew anyone who could do the test for me. She said she could do it. Her office was just around the block, three buildings down. When I arrived she was with a patient. She told him that it was important that she saw me immediately and asked him if could wait in the lobby. She waived for me to come on in. She closed the door and got a plastic bag out of her desk drawer. She asked me to turn my chair around so I had my back to her. I could feel her part my hair and pull a few. When I turned around she was putting my hair in the plastic bag. She told me she had to send it to a lab. It would take a couple of weeks to get the results. She said she was sorry but had to charge me seventy-five dollars. That was her cost for the lab report. I told her I understood and appreciated it. I already knew what the results were going to be.

During the next couple of weeks, the fraud cases kept coming. The money I had gotten from selling my interest in the penthouse was now gone. I was really stressing. It had gotten so bad that at the end of the day, my hands were shaking so bad I could not even write my own name. I was at work and went up front to see Mom. I asked her what to do.

"Don't worry, doll. I'll find a way to buy out your interest in the farm."

It wasn't much money, but it did help a lot. I had the check a couple of days later. At that moment, for the first time in my life, I realized my net worth was less than zero. I put the check into my operating account. As I wrote the date on the deposit slip, it dawned on me that it had been over a year since Gregory left me in this hell. Surely it was coming to an end now. I could only pray the suffering would pass.

The phone rang one day at the office. It was Dr. Martha. She had the test results and wanted me to drop what I was doing to come to her office. When I arrived her waiting room was full, and she had a patient in her office. She had him wait outside and flagged me in. She shut the door. The anguish in her eyes told me all I needed to know. I had definitely been poisoned. She showed me the results on a colored chart. It showed positive for arsenic. Her words were muffled by my inner thoughts wrestling with it all. It was like something you would see on TV, not in Gulf Shores. We only had four red lights. Everyone knew everyone. I muttered thanks and went back to my office to call Agent Kellie.

When I called the lady on the other end of the phone said Agent Kellie had been transferred to another case. I was sorry to hear that because he had always been so nice to me. She said I had a new agent and transferred me. The agent on the end said my case had already been transferred again to Agent Scott. He said he would transfer me, and so he did. Agent Scott answered the phone, and I told him who I was. He said he had already looked through my file and was up to date. I told him about the arsenic and the forensic hair test. He gave me his fax number and told me to fax him a copy, which I did. He let me know he would review it and get back with me in the next week or so. I thanked him and hung up the phone.

First thing the next morning, I got a call from Beau at the insurance commissioner's office. She announced that she would make a formal visit next Wednesday at ten. She suggested it would be a good idea to have my attorney present. I felt persecuted as I called to let Judge Kevin know the meeting date. He blocked out the whole morning so we could meet before and after we met Beau. I felt sick to my stomach. I broke out in a light sweat as I tried to imagine what they could possibly be coming after me for. I didn't take anyone's money. I prayed I wasn't going to jail.

THE INSURANCE
INVESTIGATION

The day finally arrived for Judge Kevin to come to my office to meet with Beau. As I was driving to work I still wondered what it could be about. After all, Gregory was the one who stole the money, not me. I would find out soon enough. I got to the office early and made myself a pot of coffee and began checking e-mails.

I was just about through when Judge Kevin walked in and took a seat in front of my desk. We sat there catching up on the latest events in our lives. Being the proud parents we were, we mostly bragged on what our kids were doing. Soon Beau came walking through the door, and we got down to business.

"Hi, I'm Beau. The insurance commissioner sent me here to try and work something out we can all live with."

"Sounds good to me, Beau."

"I've completed my investigation, and I've been instructed to make my negotiations with your attorney. Do you have somewhere the two of us can have our meeting?"

"Sure. Just take my office. I'll be right outside if you need me." I got up and closed the door behind me as I left.

I sat there for over an hour before they emerged. They were chatting it up and laughing like they were old friends as they exited my office. I couldn't think of anything that would be funny and wanted Beau to leave so I could talk to Judge Kevin, in private.

"Everything is going to be okay. I have to get back to my office to start the negotiation with the insurance department's attorney. I'll be in touch," he said. They left together before I could even get a word in.

What were you were doing in my office for the last hour then? I thought. I wasn't feeling much comfort from his words. It seemed simple enough to me. I didn't do anything wrong so what was there to negotiate.

You see, even though I did nothing wrong, the insurance department held me responsible. After all, it was my insurance company, and I was the president. It did not matter that Gregory tried to murder me. It didn't matter either that I lay at death's door for over five months. Now the insurance commission wanted to do me in the rest of the way. It was still my fault. You will find that crooks run this world—one kind or another.

A week or so went by before Judge Kevin called me to let me know he had worked out a deal with the insurance department. He wanted to see me so he could explain what they had come up with. I went to his office in Foley thinking I was good to go.

When I arrived I walked inside and saw his secretary, Amy, sitting behind the front desk. She was smiling and humming some little tune.

"Take a seat. Judge Kevin will be with you as soon as he gets off the phone. How about a cup of coffee while you wait?"

"Sure, chick, I'd love one," I graciously replied.

Amy poured me a cup and handed it to me. A few minutes later, Judge Kevin came up front. Silently he motioned me back to his chambers. I sat in front of his desk as he told me what he thought I wanted to hear. He handed me an agreement to sign. As I started to read it over, the good deal he had gotten me was no good deal at all. The insurance department had agreed to suspend my insurance license for a year.

"Dude, you know as well as I do that no license means no income. No income for a month and I go under. You might as well let them come lock the doors now. Screw it. I'll take my chances at trial!" My leg bounced up and down uncontrollably.

Judge Kevin's face turned beet red.

"Look, Wynona, I worked really hard to get them to let you keep your license. I know you don't like it, but it's the best deal they would give you."

"My daddy would roll over in his grave if I signed that crap you just handed me." I slung the papers he wanted me to sign on his desk and stood up. "That say's I did something wrong, and you know otherwise. I'm not going to let them smear my name without a fight."

"Then I can't help you anymore," he said as he twisted back and forth in his chair.

"Don't worry, Judge Kevin. I'll find someone who isn't afraid to defend the innocent. Thanks for nothing!" I blew through his office like a hurricane as I left.

As I peeled out of the parking lot, I wondered what I was going to do. I decided to call Chickee, my older sister, for some ideas. I explained to her the great deal Judge Kevin had offered me.

"Okay, now tell me the good part again," she said.

Chickee had read an article in the paper about an attorney in Prattville, Alabama, who specialized in insurance cases.

"Let me look up his number, and I'll give you a call back in a few minutes," she said.

The man's name was Mark. I immediately called him from my cell phone and made my way back to the office. We set up a meeting for the next week.

Chickee and I loaded up to cruise the three-hour ride to Mark's office in Prattville. When we arrived he was already there waiting for us. We went to his office and sat down. I filled Mark in on the details regarding my case. He listened intently as I spewed out everything that happened over the last two years.

He finally stopped my babbling and said, "Wynona, I think I can be of help to you. I can't work for free, but I'll only charge you five thousand dollars to see you through trial. If you agree, I'll contact their attorney and get started."

I gladly accepted his offer. I would have to come up with more of what I didn't have—money, but at least I was being offered some hope. Things were looking up.

I was getting nervous as the weeks passed before Mark finally called me.

"I've been back and forth with their attorney. They won't budge. I explained to them that taking your license would be like giving you the death sentence. Since we couldn't come to an agreement, we have a trial date set. The trial will be in front of a judge, not a jury. I want you to line up some people who will testify for you," he said.

"No worries. I'll be more than ready. You just tell me anything else you need me to do, and I'll get it done. Thanks so much for your help, Mark."

After I got off the phone, I started calling the clients I thought might be willing to help me. I quickly lined up twelve. I figured that would be enough. Everybody I called said yes. I was confident I'd be vindicated.

My anxiety built over the next few months as we waited for the trial date to get here. It was finally time to go to Mobile to the federal courthouse. Some of the clients met me at the office to follow me over. Some met us at the hotel restaurant next door to the courthouse.

Mark was sitting at the restaurant waiting for us to arrive. We all sat down at a long table and had breakfast. There was Pastor Roy, Bruce the retired FBI agent, Patty the hairdresser, Harry the contractor, Dr. Martha, and more. When we finished eating breakfast, Mom and Mark argued over the check. Mom finally won and went to pay.

We all walked inside the courthouse together. Beside the metal detector inside, there was a handmade sign that read "Pamela Wynona Schoen, Room 206." What a hoot that was. I was so important they had to give people directions to the event. Patty made me stand by the sign and took my picture with her cell phone. We laughed all the way to the elevators. Once we got on the elevator to go upstairs to the courtroom, I felt the walls closing in on me. I wondered if I would be in a jail cell the size of the elevator cab for the next few years. When the cab stopped, I pushed my way out ahead of the others. I had chills as we walked toward the courtroom.

Once inside we all sat on the left side of the courtroom, except Brother Roy. He sat on the right side behind the insurance department's attorney. Having my little angel looking over their shoulder put me at ease. In the back of the room was the press-register reporter that had been writing about my troubles since the story broke. I knew things were bad for me when Alabama beat Auburn for the first time in six years, and we both made the front page. I knew it was really bad when the game took up two columns and the one on me took up four. How about that?

The judge came out, and the trial began. The insurance department presented its case first, and their attorney called their first witness. It was Beau, the investigator. She stayed on the stand for two hours. I didn't think her testimony was that damaging. Next was a lady I had written a homeowner's policy for. She actually testified that I had paid her back. I was home free. Next was another client I had never heard of, and she testified to the same. The fourth witness was a young man. He was not in my corner. He said he had called the office several times to get a refund and that I had never called him back. He was the only one. I never got his messages. Of course their last witness was the man from Elberta who had started the whole thing. His testimony supported me. When I found out that his policy had been faked by Gregory, I gave him a full refund, as he requested. I really did not think they had a very good case against me.

The judge called for a lunch recess and dismissed us for two hours. When we came back, it was our turn. The judge asked my witnesses to wait outside. He would call them in one by one.

First on the stand was Bruce. They swore him in, and Mark began our case.

"Sir, can you tell the court what happened when you purchased insurance from the defendant?" Mark asked.

"Well, my wife and I went to Wynona to take out a homeowner's policy. She wrote us a policy, and we paid a year's premium. When it hit the paper about the fraud, we read her ad she posted and called her to see if our policy was good or not. She let us know that it was not good and asked us come by to see her so that she could make things right."

"What did you do then?" Mark asked.

"Well, we set up a time to meet at her office. When we got there, she asked if we wanted a refund or another policy. We told her that a new policy would be fine. She wrote us a new policy on the spot and paid for the policy with her money," he replied.

"Is there anything else you can tell the court?"

"Yes, sir. Wynona isn't guilty of anything. We trust her. She's a lady whose word is good!"

"Thank you, sir. No further questions, Your Honor," he concluded as he sat down at the defense table.

The insurance attorney, Lisa, stood up. "I have no questions for this witness, Your Honor."

Bruce got up and walked outside the courtroom to be with the other witnesses.

Next was Harry. I did not know what Harry would say and had debated for days on whether I should ask him to come or not. I finally decided to take a chance.

"Would you explain for the court your dealings with the defendant?" Mark asked.

"I bought insurance on my house and a rental house I own. When I found out what was happening, I called to see if mine were frauds, also. Unfortunately, neither were any good. I went to see her, and she wrote me two new polices, and she paid the premiums."

"No further questions," Mark said.

Mark sat down and Lisa stood up. "No questions," she said again.

Harry left the stand to go back outside with the others.

Next was Pastor Roy.

"How did you find out that your polices were no good?"

"I was at my office when she called me to let me know what Gregory had done. She asked me to stop by so she could make it right. So I stopped in, and she wrote me a new policy and paid my premium for me," Pastor Roy said.

"Thank you, sir. No further questions."

Again Lisa stood and dismissed the witness without questioning him. When he left the stand, he sat back down behind the prosecutor's table.

Next they called Dr. Martha. She walked into the courtroom and took the stand. They swore her in, and she sat down.

"Doctor, please tell the court your association with the defendant," Mark said.

"I've been her client for a while. One day I called to speak with her, and Gregory answered her office phone. He told me that she was out sick and that he would be glad to help me. I told him that I would only speak with Wynona about my insurance. He gave me her cell number so I could call her."

"What else happened?" Mark asked her.

"Well, Wynona told me she didn't feel good but she would come to the office to take care of me. I purchased my homeowner's policy and paid my down payment. I think it was for three months. After that I got a bill in the mail from her insurance company to renew my policy. I mailed my check in and thought nothing of it until the story about the fraud hit the news. I called to see if my policy was good or not. She checked and let me know I needed to come by so she could write me a new one because it was no good. Gregory had taken the premium that I mailed in for himself. I came in, and she proceeded to write me a good policy, and she paid the premium that was due."

"Is there anything else relevant to this case you can add?"

"Yes, sir. When she came to my office, I noticed some troubling purple marks on her arms and elbows. I told her right then that I was certain she had been poisoned. Before I became a doctor, I was a nurse for ten years. During that time we had to take a class two days a year for arsenic training. I told her that arsenic had collected in her joints and that's what was causing her elbow to become purple. I sent a hair sample to a lab, and the results confirmed my diagnosis. I suggested she take a detox pill. She would need to eat fresh greens every day and walk as much as possible. I told her she could no longer eat seafood. Eventually, she will suffer from extreme arthritis that won't go away," she told the court.

"No more questions. Your witness." He sat down.

Lisa couldn't excuse her from the stand quick enough. "No questions here, Your Honor," she blurted out.

Dr. Martha left the witness stand and joined the others in the hallway.

When Dr. Martha sat down, Judge Fluff spoke up.

"I believe we have had enough testimony for today. Court is adjourned until nine a.m. tomorrow," he said as he struck his gavel on the bench.

Everyone said thank you as Judge Fluff left to go to his chambers.

There were still other witnesses sitting outside the courtroom waiting for their turn to tell their story. It was a great disappointment to all the ones that sat there all day waiting. I had a lot of support from family and friends. It was great to know that some people still cared. Thank God for that.

The next day Mom and I headed back to Mobile. We met Mark for breakfast at the same spot. This time Mom let Mark pay. Once we got to the courtroom, we took our seat. Judge Fluff came out of the back and court started. First they called Mom. After swearing her in and getting her to state her name for the record, Mom took a deep breath before the questioning started.

"Do you know if Wynona stole any of her clients' money?" Mark rested his hand on hers as he waited for her reply.

"No. It was only Gregory that did that. Wynona stayed in bed sick as death for five months. Gregory had convinced her she was sick from spider bites. That's when most of her money went missing, according to the bank statements I've seen."

"Do you know what made Wynona so sick?" he asked.

"Gregory was putting something in her coffee or food they gave her," Mom said.

"How do you know she was being poisoned?" Mark asked.

"She had some kind of hair test, and it came back positive. It had to be him. He wanted her out of the office. Wynona is a smart cookie. She would have caught on sooner if she had been able to go to work every day. But she couldn't."

Mark finished his questions and let Lisa cross-examine her. Lisa did her best to trip Mom up on the details of her testimony. Mom is a sharp ole bird and never wavered in her statements. Lisa realized pretty quick that Mom wasn't going to miss a step and gave up, dismissing Mom.

As Mom left the stand, she looked at the judge with a smile and told him, "My daughter is no crook."

Next Mark called me to the stand. I had no idea I would be there three hours answering questions. They had me state my name for the record and swore me in. I did my best to settle in to the chair, but I couldn't find a comfortable position. I pulled my hair away from my face and waited for the first question.

"How long have you been selling insurance?"

"I worked for Alfa for about twenty-six years. I decided at that point to open up my own agency. I made a deal with Alabama Insurance Agency to open a franchise under their name. I was supposed to be my own boss. After a year and a half, the company owner quit paying me the commissions I earned. I parted ways with him and opened Starfish Insurance Agency. I have owned that company for the last four years. So, three decades, roughly."

"Can you explain to the court why you sell insurance?" he asked.

"Since I was two, I always wanted to sell insurance like my daddy. As I grew up around him, I saw how Daddy helped people. Everyone respected him, and I wanted to be just like him," I answered.

"How did you handle the fraud cases when you found out about them?"

"By writing them new policies if they so chose and paying their premiums. If they didn't want to do that, I gave them a full refund. If their polices were more expensive than before, I covered it all. I also took out an ad in the paper to notify people about what happened. Many I called before they found out. I did everything I could to make it right."

"How many cases were there?" he continued.

"To the best of my knowledge, there were one hundred and seventy-six." My makeup slid down my face like a California mudslide. I took a couple of tissues from the judge's desk and wiped up the mess.

"How has your lifestyle changed since this tragedy?"

I tried to gather myself as I answered. "I had everything before Gregory—a nice house, a nice Hummer. I got to take great vacations with my son. I used to be able to help others in need—friends as well as others. Now I drive a ten-year-old truck. I've lost all of my property, lost all my savings. Those things pale in comparison to how it has affected my son. He's lost everything, too. Currently he lives with his father because

I don't have the means to support him. I gave up everything to make it right with my clients. It's what my daddy would have done. It's not fair that my son has to suffer for the actions of a lowlife thief like Gregory." I wailed uncontrollably.

"No more questions."

Lisa jumped from her seat and began her attack. "Do you recognize these two business cards?" she asked, passing them to me.

"Yes. They are the cards that Gregory had made for us," I said.

"How can you tell from them who owns the company?"

"You can't. Mine was supposed to have my title under my name. When we first got the cards, I told Gregory about the omission. He blamed it on the print shop. He said we might as well use them until they ran out. Since I had already paid for them, I agreed. I had planned that I'd have it corrected on the next order. After that I never gave it a second thought. So many people in town have known me and my family a long time and already knew that I owned my company. It existed before Gregory came along," I shot back.

Lisa laid a copy of a condo magazine in front of me. In the magazine was a short article about my little company. There was a photo of myself. It stated in the text "We shop everyone's insurance rates to find the best price."

"How much did you pay for this AD?"

"Nothing at all. The reporter asked if he could do a feature on me at no cost. Kind of a local girl helping local people. I told him sure. You can't beat free publicity."

"How much did you pay for the advertising?" she asked again.

I leaned forward as far as I could. "Nothing at all. It was a *freebie*."

"Okay. So how much did you pay for the AD?"

Now I was pissed. "Nothing. It was *free*," I said through gritted teeth.

"You still haven't told me how much you paid for the AD."

"What part of *free* don't you understand? You can ask me that question a hundred more times, and the answer is still gonna be the same. I got all day. If you want to waste time asking the same question over and over, then fine. We'll sit here all day. The answer is nothing—free, no charge. Get it!"

Judge Fluff raised his voice at Lisa. "I've had enough of you badgering the defendant. She has answered you multiple times. Her answer is that she received the AD at no cost. Move on, or we are done here. The defendant is correct: you are wasting my time!"

Lisa, embarrassed, told him, "Yes, sir. I'll move on."

"Did Gregory have an insurance license?"

"No."

"Why then would you allow him to sell insurance policies to clients?" she demanded.

"I didn't. Gregory's job was to take the payments to the bank and write receipts. He was also responsible for keeping up with my accounting. That was it. Nothing else. Had I ever known what he was up to, I can assure you and the court I would have put a stop to it immediately."

"Did you ever tell anyone that Gregory was an agent for you?"

"I just told you I didn't," I countered.

"Did you ever see or hear him tell anyone that he was an insurance agent for your company?" she asked again.

"You are on thin ice again, counselor. Move on," Judge Fluff said.

"Did Gregory ever tell you he had a master's degree in accounting?" Lisa asked.

"Yes."

"Did you ever try to confirm it?" she inquired.

"I didn't because I trusted him. He showed the skills of someone with an accounting degree. His mom stated to me when we met that he had the degree. But no, I never contacted the university to get a copy of his diploma. Who would?"

"Did you call any of his former employers to see if they would recommend him?"

"No, I never called anyone. However, I went to a Christmas party at the furniture store that he worked at before he came to work for me. Gregory had invited me when his mom worked for me. His employer came over to all of us and bragged to Gregory's mom that he was the hardest-working, honest person she had ever met. She told her she couldn't get by with out him. When he came to work for me, that was all I needed."

"At what time did you put up a webpage hiring agents in other states to write policies for you?" she demanded.

"Never. Gregory was responsible for that also. I didn't know about it until one day I got a call, after he had gone on the lamb, from a woman in Texas. She told me she was one of my agents. I told her I didn't have any agents. She said she found me on the Internet under insurance brokers. I looked online while she was still on the phone. She was right. Gregory had posted a picture of my office with Gregory's name as the owner. The site charged a fee of seven hundred dollars for the right to write policies under my company name. I told her it was a scam. I also explained what Gregory had pulled with my clients' money and that he was still on the run. The reason she was calling was that a policy she had written her customer had turned up as a fraud. Her client turned her into the Texas Insurance Commissioner. She had paid Gregory cash. She asked me to return the amount she had given him. I agreed minus the commission she had been paid. I mailed the check that same day." My bladder was pulsing, I had to go pee so bad. I found a new position and hoped it was better than the last.

Finally, Lisa couldn't come up with any relevant questions. Judge Fluff excused me from the witness stand.

"I will review the evidence in this case and will contact your attorney within two weeks with my decision. I knew your daddy, Wynona, and I know he would be proud of you. I will be as fair as the law will allow. And by the way, you have a very colorful range of clients. Court is adjourned," he announced.

I told Judge Fluff as I was leaving the stand, "That's nothing. I only handpicked a few, and thank you for the kind words about Daddy."

Mom, Mark, and I walked out of the courtroom. Mark said he was going back to college to get a special degree in law. I was his last case for now. He wanted me to know that what happened had not been my fault.

"I had a legal secretary a few years ago who worked for me for three years. She also balanced my books for me. I'd check my books every month and never found anything wrong. I was working a case and the court date got postponed till the following month. I went back to the office to get some research done on another case. When I got to the office my secretary was out running errands. The phone rang, and I answered it. On the other end was a lady who wanted to reschedule her and her husband's divorce. I checked my calendar, and their names weren't there. I put her on hold and went to my secretary's appointment book. There they were in black and white. I told her I'd get back to her within an hour. I compared her appointment book to mine, and it blew me away. There were dozens of clients on hers, but not on mine. She had been seeing people behind my back for years. I fired her. She didn't do anytime or anything. There is no way to know how many people from Montgomery County who are still married and think they aren't. I'll call you as soon as I hear from Judge Fluff."

Mom and I got in the car and made the hour ride back to the office.

It had been almost two years, and still Gregory had not been caught. Business was picking up, and I had started making a good living again. Two weeks later the phone rang at work, and it was Mark.

"Hey, Wynona. I finally got the verdict from Judge Fluff. Are you sitting down?"

"Yeah, yeah, I'm sitting down. What did it say? Did he find me not guilty, or what?"

I tried hard not to faint as he spoke. I crossed my fingers.

"I did the best I could. I'm sorry. I wish we could have gotten you that verdict. I really do. It's not too bad, though, considering. The judge let you keep your license. He's ordered you to pay a thirty-six-thousand-dollar fine and eighteen months of unsupervised probation."

"Is that really all? So no jail, and I keep my license?"

"That's right. He also has a special condition of his ruling. He's making it mandatory that you take a class to learn the QuickBooks program."

I almost laughed when he told me that. I stopped being mad at the judge and smiled for the first time since I saw the sign in the courthouse with my name on it.

"That's just too funny."

"It also states that if you pay the fine and take the accounting class you can get off probation sooner. It's not all that bad. It's just a little expensive. I'll fax you over a copy to study. Send me back your signed copy back to me sometime next week. Congratulations again, Wynona. Bye."

I wasn't vindicated, and my name wasn't cleared, but I still had my license to do what I was called in life to do. Sell insurance.

A few days later my copy of the verdict came in the mail. It said exactly what Mark had told and faxed me. I went to the bank and got a cashier's check for six thousand. At the time that was all I could afford to send them. I would have to make payments until I paid off my fine. One good thing about it: if I finished my requirements before the deadline, the state would do a final audit and close my case. With all the court drama, I was way behind on my work and hired Mary to be my second bookkeeper. Mary worked for years as an auditor for Blue Cross Blue Shield, but best of all, she volunteered to help me for free. With her help, and Lou's, we were catching up fast.

A month later I got a letter in the mail saying they were having a two-day QuickBooks seminar in Pensacola, Florida. I decided we all should go and got us signed up. When we went I was bored after the first fifteen minutes. I was stuck for two days. I just prayed I did not fall asleep in class. The days passed quicker than I thought they would. We finished and picked up our completion certificates. All I had to do now was fax them to the state insurance department. The next day it was back to work.

I had been at work a couple of hours when I got a call from Judge Kevin. He had been keeping up with my case and was taking it back over until all the loose ends had been taken care of. I thought that was great. I would not owe him any money because I had already paid him. He let me know he was going to send an e-mail to Lisa and let her know she needed to go through him. I thanked him and hung up. The rest of the work day went by fast. It was time to go home and rest.

THE IRS

The next day I got to work thinking things were looking up when in walked a man in a suit. He came back
to my office and gave me his business card. His name
was Smidley from the IRS. He said I had made the
paper one time too many and had caught his boss's eye.
He was there to do an audit. I had always paid my taxes
and had never been through an audit. I can tell you it
ain't fun.

Once you get on their hit list, I do not think you
ever get off. Smidley asked if I had employees or subcontractors. I said subcontractors. He asked if they had
set hours. I said yes. He said I was wrong. If they had
set hours, they were employees. I was responsible for
the payroll taxes, which I had not been paying. He said
currently I owed $140,000. I tried not to cry.

"You've done the audit. Now where do you suppose
I'm going to come up with that kind of money?"

"Look. If you don't pay, I have the authority to lock
your doors until you do."

"That doesn't make any sense. If you lock my doors,
I won't have any way to pay."

"Ma'am, we're the IRS. We aren't required to make sense. Now here's the list of the paperwork you will need for our meeting next week. I would make sure everything is there before you show up."

I was not in the mood for this guys' attitude. Unfortunately, it's unlawful to go redneck on an IRS agent.

"I'll have it together by the end of the day. There is no way I owe that kind of money. Why is it I have to pay on money you guys know Gregory stole? It's absurd!"

"Oh, don't worry. I'll deal with Gregory in due course. See you next week."

What a jerk, I thought. After he was gone, I turned to the girls.

"Looks like I'm going to war with the IRS. See if we have all the documents they have requested. Let me know what's missing so I can round it up. I'm going into my office to vent." I slammed my door behind me and blocked the world outside for a while. *Lord, grant me patience.*

The next week I called Smidley's office. He answered the phone, and I told him my name. I was trying to explain the reason for my call when he burst into a fit of laughter.

"I don't find anything amusing about being audited by the IRS. Do you want to let me in on the joke?"

"I'm sorry, Wynona. I was just remembering the stressed-out look on your face the day I came to see you. It's really not going to be as bad as you think. Fax me over the paperwork, and you won't have to come by this week. We'll just get together next week. And relax. It will be okay."

"Well, you aren't the one with your head on the chopping block. I'll see you next week."

He continued to laugh; I hung up the phone. I wished the target on my back would vanish. Gregory has been on the run for two years. I needed them to catch him. I needed peace. I shut it all out and thought about Little Dude.

Little Dude was growing up way to fast. He had decided to play city league basketball for the last time. He was now fourteen years old. He was six foot, skinny as a rail, and good looking. He looked just like his mom (redneck humor). I bet those little chicks drove him crazy. He had a girlfriend for the first time that I was aware of. Her parents were clients of mine. They would stop by from time to time to give me an update on the courtship. He never would tell me anything about her. All he would say was everything was fine.

Tryouts started in Orange Beach. It was for ages thirteen and fourteen. They had enough players for two teams. The coaches both got their sons on their team. Now it was time to pick the players. First up was Coach Floyd. He had watched Little Dude the year before. When they finished Little Dude was the only fourteen-year-old on his team. All his friends had been picked by Orange Beach 2.

I was sitting in my pickup truck waiting on Little Dude to come out so we could go home. Coach Floyd came over to the truck and was all excited. Little Dude was getting in the truck as Coach Floyd was walking off. He had a long, sad face. I asked him why the blues. He said all his friends were on the other team, and he wanted to play with them. I said he need not worry. He would just shine like a star. We cranked up and went home.

The first game was the following week. It was Orange Beach 1 against Orange Beach 2. That game Little Dude looked like a one-dude team, but it was not enough. They lost to the other Orange Beach team. Little Dude was disappointed. I told him not to worry. They could beat them next time. As the season progressed, Little Dude improved. Every Saturday he would meet his friends at the recreation center and play basketball until they closed. They played several more games and had started winning. It was time to play Orange Beach 2 again. Little Dude was not looking forward to it.

The game started and Little Dude was scoring. At halftime they were ahead. Benjamin Overton was a friend of Little Dude's and was on the other team. Little Dude was not only scoring but was a great blocker, too. Right before halftime, Little Dude blocked Benjamin for the sixth time. Bent old Little Dude to quit. Little Dude told him no. Ben said they were friends. Little Dude just laughed and said he was there to win. The final score was 50–30. Little Dude's team had won. The fourth quarter Little Dude did not score. Every time he got the ball he would throw it to another player.

After the game I asked him why he hadn't tried to score in the last quarter. He said he had scored enough and wanted his teammates to have a chance to score. I thought I had done a real good job as a single parent raising my child. Little Dude went to get his gym bag. A dad from the other team came up to me. He said next time they played against Little Dude, he was going to put blinders on him. He laughed and said never mind. Little Dude would still make the shots. A mother from the other team came up to me. Little Dude and her son, Zan, had been best friends for years. She asked me what I fed him. I said nothing before the game. He would never eat until afterward. She was smiling as she walked away. Next came my friend Doris. Her son, Mickey, was on the other team. She said she had told Mickey before the game to break Little Dude's leg as soon as he got on the court. I told her that was being a bad parent. Doris just started laughing. She said it was not fair that Little Dude was not on her son's team.

The following week was my appointment with Smidley. Even though Lou had been there for only a short time, she decided to go with me and take notes.

It was another blistering sunny southern day. Lou and I got in her van to make the IRS appointment. When we arrived, Smidley was standing in the lobby waiting for us. I introduced Lou as we walked down the long hallway to his office. When we all sat down, Smidley looked at me and smiled.

"Honey, I have some great news for you. The amount you owe the IRS has been reduced."

Jubilation ripped through my veins. Then I came back to reality.

"When you say reduced, how much are we talking about?"

"Drastically reduced—from a hundred and forty thousand to twenty-six."

"Dollars?"

"Twenty-six thousand dollars. You owe the IRS for thirteen quarters worth of taxes. That's the total of the payments you missed. You pay those, and you are free and clear with us."

"That's great, but I'm still broke. You are going to lock my doors just the same. It might as well be ten million."

"Only if you don't settle up. That's just the way it works."

I owed four years of taxes even though the accounting firm in Gulf Shores had done my taxes for years. He told Lou to write down the payments along with the quarter and year they belonged to so she did.

With a heavy heart, I stood up to leave. I had cashed in all my life insurance, sold all my property that I could, and borrowed all the money I had laying around. I called Mom on the cell phone. I asked her what I was to do. She said she would call Chickee and see about borrowing some money out of the trust.

The next day at work Chickee called. She said she and Baby Doll had discussed it. Instead of borrowing money from the trust, I could just borrow the money out of one of Mom's life insurance policies. I agreed. When it came time for me to meet Baby Doll at her office, I found out something different. Baby Doll and Chickee had decided to sign over their interest in one of Mom's policies. I was to give up my interest in two others. What a deal for them.

It was only supposed to take seven days to get my money. While waiting on it to arrive, the phone rang. It was Agent Bob. He said I needed to be in his office in two hours. Mind you this time he did not ask. He just told me. I said I would be there. Mom and I got in her car and cruised over to Mobile. We arrived at the federal building and walked inside. We took the elevator to the second floor where Agent Bob's office was. We walked to the door that lead to his office. There was a button on the left side of the door that said Push. I did and a voice asked me what my business was. I told her I had an appointment with Agent Bob. A minute later the door opened, and Agent Bob was standing there smiling. He asked us to come on in. He told Mom to take a seat and for me to follow him to the back.

Behind the lobby door that led to the back were a dozen agents dressed in suits with guns. We walked down the hallway to a room with no windows. He took me inside and told me to have a seat. He then explained to me that he had sent the arsenic report to their doctor. The doctor had looked at it and told him it was not arsenic. He said it was because I ate seafood. I just looked at Agent Bob in disbelief. I told him he better get a new doctor, that the one they used needed to go back to college. He said he was the best in the country. I told him I reckon not.

Agent Bob started asking me questions. When he was finished, he wanted to know if I would come back and take a lie detector test. I said he could hook me up. He said he could not at the moment because they did not have the machine there. He would make the arrangements and call me. He told me he had dudes tell him that before and pull a no-show. It cost the federal government money and if I was not really going to come to tell him now. I just looked at him and said I may be a redneck but my word meant a lot to me. The secret service had to fly someone down to administer the test. He said he would be in touch, and he unlocked the door to led me back to the lobby. Mom and I cruised back to the office where she dropped me to get my truck.

The next day I went back to work. It had been seven days since I had signed the paperwork on the life insurance. I was wondering where my check was. My deadline was drawing near, and I was getting nervous. I decided to call ALFA Insurance Company and find out where my money was. I spoke with Mandy in the loan department. She informed me they had not sent it as of yet. Just my luck. If I ever got any good news, I would probably just drop dead of a heart attack. Every day was just one more lame adventure. If life gives you lemons make lemonade. I had learned in the last several years to drink a lot of lemonade.

Two days later I called Mandy back.

"Hey, chick, this is Wynona calling. I still haven't gotten a check. Can you help me find out why? The IRS is breathing down my neck like there is no tomorrow."

"Sure. Hold on." I was on hold for almost fifteen minutes.

"I'm sorry, Wynona. Somehow the checks got approved but never got written. I made sure they were in the envelope before I got back on the phone with you. They will arrive overnight."

"Geez. Okay. Thanks, Mandy. I'll call you when they get here."

The weight of the world bore down on me.

The next day Mom checked her mail. It wasn't there. Instead they had sent it overnight to my company physical address. When it arrived I was shocked. I thought my luck was finally looking up. I took it to my local bank and deposited it into my operating account. The teller informed me that because it was over five thousand, they had to put a hold on it for seven days. More good news.

When I got back, I called Smidley with a heavy heart. He answered the phone, and I told him what had happened. He said he would put a note in my file. He was fine with it as long as he knew it was coming. I asked him how he wanted me to get it to him. He told me to write thirteen different checks. When I could transfer the money out just to buzz him and let him know. I hung up the phone for another busy day at the office. It was like every other day.

The phone never stopped. People just dropped by. I hardly ever left the office to go to lunch. I would try to eat at the office. Between the phone ringing and people coming by, it usually took me three hours to eat. They were never big meals either. I had been trying to gain some weight. I had been malnourished since Gregory tried to murder me. I was doing better. I was up to eating three small meals a day. The little purple dots that were showing up on my face, arms, legs, and stomach had been getting less and less. I still had to stay out of the sun and watch what I ate. Every time I stayed outside too long, I would get lightheaded and do some more refunding.

The next day I met Mom at the office. We loaded up in her car to drive to Mobile to see Agent Bob. It was the day I was going to take the lie detector test and finally prove I was innocent. I could hardly wait. It was a nice drive over, and we were both quiet. I was thinking about what kind of questions they were going to ask me. I just wanted it to be over. I was tried of being reminded of Gregory and what he had done to me.

We got there and took the elevator to the second floor. I pushed the button to let them know I was there. I was right on time. A few seconds later, the door opened and there stood Agent Bob. He was smiling as usual and told Mom to take a seat and for me to come on back. We went to the same little room with no windows. There sitting at the small table was a new agent. Agent Michael was from Chicago. He explained that normally he did not get involved unless it involved one hundred million dollars or more. I asked why he bothered with my case. Gregory had not stolen anywhere close to that. He said because they asked. I think it had to do with Gregory's third indictment. He had two because of me. During their investigation Agent Bob had uncovered something else Gregory had done. He would not tell me.

Michael was in his early forties. Tall, good looking, and he wore a very expensive suit. Not an ounce of fat on him. To say he was easy on the eyes was an understatement. Agent Michael asked me to take a seat at the table in the middle of the room. A single bulb hung above it. On the table was a laptop. It had all sorts of wires coming out of it that led to another chair off in the corner of the room. Next to the chair in the corner was a large metal box sitting on another table. Agent Michael sat in the chair behind the lap top. I sat across the table from him. I kept looking at the chair in the corner as he began.

"Let's get started by getting a little background info, okay?"

"Fire away!" I sat there with my back straight and looking forward.

"Would you say you had a good childhood?"

"Sure. Mom and Dad saw to all our needs. We had horses, played tennis, swam competitively, and even took ballet lessons. We took two family vacations every year. They also raised us in the church where we learned right from wrong. I'd say I had a great childhood."

"Have you ever stolen anything?"

"Yes, sir. Before I could read, I was at a store with my mom. There were some toy rings in a box on the counter, and I put one on my finger before we left. Mom found out when we got home, and I got a serious spanking. She made me go back with her to the store and apologize to the owner for taking the ring. I think I was five."

"That doesn't count. Later when I ask you if you have ever stolen anything just say no. Have you ever lied to anyone?"

"Yes. My mom when I was sixteen."

"That doesn't count either. Again, when I ask that question later, your answer will be no. Okay?"

"Got it."

"Have you ever stolen any of your clients' money?"

"Never."

"Just yes or no."

"No."

"Have you ever faxed proof of insurance to a bank knowing the policy was fake?"

"No."

Agent Michael asked me to go sit in the chair in the corner. I was to put my feet on the black square metal thing on the floor. He then hooked up my index finger. He attached six different wires to my arms and back. He told me to sit still and look forward. I could not even cough. I wondered if he was going to let me still breathe or if I had to hold my breath, too. He went and took his seat. He turned on his computer, and the test started. I tapped my finger on the arm of my chair.

"Please don't do that. Sit there perfectly still. Don't blink or cough, okay? We are going to start the test now."

"Okay." I tried to relax and took a deep breath as he began again.

"Have you ever stolen anything in your life?"

My heart raced. Then I remembered he said the ring didn't count. I exhaled slowly.

"No."

"Have you ever lied to anyone in your life?"

I breathed deeply.

"No."

"Have you ever stolen money from your clients?"

"No." I tried not to look at anything—just space.

"Have you ever issued fraudulent insurance policies to anyone?"

"No." The room was misty as I listened to each question.

It continued for nearly an hour. Over and over he questioned me. Except for needing to visit the ladies' room, I was relaxed and at ease. He asked me the same questions as before. The test only took five or six minutes. He got up to unhook me. He asked me to come back to the table for the results. He called in Agent Bob first.

"Well, how did she do?"

"That one there isn't guilty of anything. And I do mean *anything*."

Agent Michael hurried to pack his torture device.

"I've got to run. Got another case elsewhere, and I have to make a flight. Good luck to you."

I felt like I was in a cheap gumshoe flick. Finally, everyone knew I was innocent, and that felt awesome! Agent Bob walked me out of the dungeon and down the hall.

"Did you know that we investigated you, Wynona?"

"Yep. If you hadn't you wouldn't have been doing your job."

"How did you know?"

"I know you hacked into my computer. You had me followed and tapped all my phones. You probably even used the cell towers to follow my cell phone. Oh, and you definitely have been keeping your eye on my bank accounts."

He looked liked I had just guessed the launch codes to of all the nukes on earth.

"Now how could a redneck possibly have picked up on all of that?"

"Dude, I watch CSI. I know what you guys do." I smiled at him. "Do you have any leads on Gregory?"

"We have a few leads but still don't have a fix on where he's hiding. He may have fled the country somehow."

"Like I told you before: when you find him, he's going to be laying low in Florida."

"I doubt it, but maybe. Let's hope we find him soon."

"Amen to that!"

Mom and I left and went back to the office to finish out our day.

After we got back, I got a cup of coffee and headed to my office. The front door opened and a lady and her son walked in. She told Mom they wanted to see me and get some car insurance. Mom told them to go on back. They walked into my office and took a seat in front of my desk. She said she had had car insurance with me before and wanted to take out a new policy. She was living on social security and her policy had lapsed. She just had not had the extra money to pay it. I was in the process of asking her some information and about her driving record and about what kind of car she had. She explained she had been following my story in the newspaper and knew I was not guilty. She wanted me to be her agent again. I was so thankful for the loyalty my clients showed me.

I picked up the phone to call Smidley. I told him the money was now available. I had made the IRS deposits like he asked me to do. He said I had misunderstood. I was supposed to mail the money straight to him. I thought what I had done was right. He said he would find the money and apply it to my account. He called a couple of days later to let me know out of thirteen checks he had only found eight. Five checks were still missing. He wanted me to fax him the deposits so he could track them down so I did. It took him five months to find my five checks. In the meantime the IRS was sending me notices for late fees and penalties. When he called me, he told me he would apply the money and the case would be closed. I asked him about the late charges. He agreed to remove them. How can the IRS lose money deposited to their account? Oh well, he did find it and that worry was finally gone. I wore my battle scars the best way I knew how: inside.

I was at work weeks later when I got a call from my girlfriend Karla. She had been keeping up on the events of what had happened to me on her computer.

"They caught him! I just looked him up online. They caught him like two weeks ago!" she screamed.

"For real, chick?"

"I swear it's true. Look it up, and call me back."

I grabbed the phone and dialed Agent Bob's number. It rang twice.

"Is it true?"

"I was just picking up the phone to tell you. Yes, we got him."

Just picking up the phone my backside.

"So where in Florida did you find him?"

He paused for a moment. *Come on, admit it,* I thought.

"Pensacola," came his dry answer. I guess crow wasn't that tasty after all.

"Is he still in jail? You better not let him post bail, or he will run."

"Yes, he's in jail. And, no, he's not going anywhere. He'll be in jail till his court date."

"When and where is the court date? I'm not going to miss it."

"You can't come."

He had lit my redneck fuse.

"I've waited years for this moment. There's no way I'm not coming. I promise you that!"

"The court will be closed. It'll just be Gregory and the judge. That's it, nobody else. I'll call and give you an update."

He smothered my burning fuse.

"Okay. Don't forget to call me please."

"I won't. I promise we'll talk soon."

I wasn't counting on him to call me. They caught him two weeks before they admitted they had him. *If I hadn't called, he wouldn't have told me squat*, I thought.

The rest of the day I could not keep my mind on work. All I could think about was that Gregory was caught and I was finally going to have my life back. He was not going to be able to enjoy the fancy clothes, cars, or vacations on me anymore. In fact, I was looking forward to having my money back so I could enjoy one—a very, very long one with Little Dude.

THE CROSSBAR MOTEL

About a week passed. I rarely saw a fraud case anymore, and life was somewhat normal. I was at my desk alone with my thoughts for a change, pouring over all that happened since the day I met Barbara and her family. I was still trying to wrap my mind around how much Gregory had stolen and what it had taken to straighten it out with my clients, the insurance commission, IRS, my creditors, and especially Mom. I lost everything I had plus my inheritance. My son lost his innocence in it all. I was well over the million mark as I calculated the losses when the phone rang. I hoped it was Agent Bob. Now that the damaged was done, there was just that one loose end—Gregory in prison.

To my dismay it was a mechanic from Pensacola.

"Hi, Wynona. I have the estimate on your Jeep ready. We need to put in a complete new wiring harness to fix all the damage. The estimate comes to three thousand nine hundred forty-seven dollars and eighteen cents. How would you like to pay? We take credit cards and debit cards, but no checks. And of course cash," he said, waiting for my reply.

I sat there for a second with my chin on my desk. Then the anger hit me. I began to answer his questions.

"Thanks for calling me. Now, I've got some questions for you, dude! How did you get my name and number? Second, what is your physical address? The finance company has been trying to repo the Jeep, and I told them if I ever found it, I'd help them get it back. As for paying you, I couldn't if I wanted to right now. Even if I could, with what has happened to me because of Barbara, Gregory, and Joshua, I'd sooner die than pay for anything else. I was so overwhelmed, I almost cried.

For a moment he was silent, and then he went on to explain how he got the Jeep. It seems the Jeep was sitting in Joshua's mom's driveway somewhere around Atmore. She let him know when he picked it up the Jeep hadn't run in over six months. When she tried to take it for a ride, it wouldn't do anything. The mechanic found that something had chewed through most of the wiring under the hood.

I gave him the condensed version of what happened when they worked for me.

"Ma'am, how about we do this. I'm familiar with the Jeep's repo guy, and I'll arrange to get it to them. You won't owe me a thing. I'm so sorry to hear what happened to you. Good luck to ya."

"Thanks, dude," I said and hung up the phone.

Unbelievable! Gregory was in lockup but his crew was still trying to clean me out. I prayed to God, "Please, Lord, let it stop. I just can't take anymore!" I was numb. But I kept going.

A couple of weeks later, I got notified that the bank sold the Jeep but not for enough to payoff the loan. Two thousand nine hundred dollars was the balance. I scrapped up the money somehow and paid them just to be completely done with it.

It had been nearly a month since I spoke with Agent Bob. I was wondering if I would hear from him when he walked in one day, unannounced. I offered him a cup of coffee and a place to rest his backside. After some idle chitchat, we got to the real reason he was there.

"I wanted to let you know that Gregory went before the federal judge yesterday. When she asked him to enter his plea, he quickly blurted out not guilty," he stated in a friendly tone.

"What a surprise."

"What I'm here for, Wynona, and you aren't going to believe this, is when the judge asked him why he had fled, he said that you have connections with the Russian mafia and that you put out a contract on him. I hate to ask, but do you have connections with the Russian Mafia, and did you ask them to kill Gregory?" He was completely serious.

If laughter could kill, I would have died right then. Mom ran back to see what was so funny. She stood there listening as we continued to talk.

"That is the funniest and yet the most absurd thing I have ever heard. You are gonna have to give me a second," I managed to get out.

Agent Bob sat there with his "I'm waiting for an answer" face.

I composed myself. "I can assure you, Agent Bob, as far as I know, I don't know anyone or anyone that knows anyone in those social circles. If I did, which I don't, I'm pretty sure that that they don't work for free. And as everyone knows, I'm flat broke."

"I'm sorry, Wynona, but it's my job to ask," he said.

"I'm going to have to remember that one for my book!" I laughed.

Agent Bob couldn't tell me anything about the case. He got up and left, and I just sat there. Depressed, I buried myself in the endless catch-up work. I thought of my son. Little Dude wouldn't admit it, but he was feeling it, too. The bubbly, funny kid I knew was barely saying anything. When he did, it was words of encouragement for me. That really got to me. I desperately wanted to give him his joyful life back.

A reporter I befriended called a couple of months later to give me the latest scoop on the court proceedings on Gregory. The prosecutor subpoenaed Gregory's husband, Joshua, to testify. On the stand Joshua told the truth about Gregory's evildoings. I thanked God that he told the truth. During that session, Gregory's attorney changed the plea to guilty. The judge, feeling overly generous, released him without bond and assigned him a probation officer to check in with monthly until his sentencing, which was scheduled two months later. The reporter let me know that sentencing would be open to the public, and I could make a statement to the court if I wanted. That was of little comfort knowing he was out of jail.

Again, even after he admitted to some of what he had done, they let him walk out of court a free man. I began to consider that he might do while he was on the street and wondered if he would come after me. He'd tried to poison me to death before. At the very least I figured he would collect up the loot and split for Mexico or Canada. Even Turkey crossed my mind. I looked for any distraction I could find to ease my fears, my anguish, my heartbreak.

Sentencing was two months away. I could hardly sleep or eat. It had been three years since I had seen him. I dreaded how it would feel after all this time to see him again. I just wanted to look him in his eyes as they read him his sentence then one last look at him from behind as they dragged him out of there in his fine orange coveralls sporting "DOC" and jingling his prison bling.

Out of the blue one day, I got a call from Mathew, Gregory's probation officer. He wanted to know if I would consider Gregory a good—or as he put it—model employee. That was the best joke I have ever heard! I mean one-liners, skits—you name it. That one wins, hands down. I honored him by laughing for about two and a half minutes. Then I tried to tell him one as funny.

Tongue in cheek, I replied, "Hmm, let's see. If you would consider committing attempted murder, fraud, embezzlement, and other crimes a model employee, then absolutely, yes. I would even recommend that, short of Judas, they give him the all-time model employee award."

Mathew just started cracking up on the phone.

"Are you familiar with the country song 'I'll Pray for You'?"

"Yes. Why do you ask?"

"I've got to pray for my brother." I laughed.

He burst into his own fit of laughter. He let me know that the sentencing date would be on the twenty-eighth the next month. When we hung up, I couldn't wait. In less than forty days, I would get my life back. My money, my ride, my houses, Mom's money—everything, especially Little Dude's carefree life. If I was lucky, they might even make him pay me interest. That would be sweet to get to go on vacation on his dime. May justice be served to the unjust.

It was the day before Gregory was to be sentenced. *Twenty four hours*, I thought, *and it's finally over*. My daydreaming was drowned out by the ringing phone on my desk. On the other end was Agent Bob. He let me know that court was the next day at one in the afternoon. I didn't let him know that I already knew.

"I don't think it's a good idea for you to see him," he said.

"Look, Bob, it's like this: You wouldn't let me sit in on the other court proceedings. I have been told that the victim has the right to make a statement at sentencing hearing. And guess what? I was the victim in this. I'm preparing a speech to give tomorrow before the judge, and I'm sure enough gonna be there to read it," I said defiantly.

"Oh, Lord! You aren't really, are you?" he said in disbelief.

"You bet I am, dude! I've waited too long for this day to come."

I hung up the phone with Agent Bob and packed my purse for the ride home. I knew that soon the bank would throw me out of the house. But I prayed after Gregory's sentencing I could pay it off again. I ached for something to shift my life back on track. As I pulled into the driveway, I was thinking of my speech. My friend Mary, Gregory's old coworker from the furniture store, was due to show up soon. She and her boyfriend and I had become good friends since we met at their Christmas party years ago. She offered to help me with the speech for the next day. She would bring her friend Kate, and we could all just chill while we worked on the speech. I had settled in on the front porch when I spotted their car coming down the drive. She always felt somewhat responsible for what happened. She once suggested that she even felt like a victim of his, too. They were just as close, but she was blind to the signs, just as I was. She considered him to be her best friend. If I hadn't come along, who knows, maybe he would have done her in, maybe even killed her.

Mary, Kate, and I walked in the house and found a spot on the couch to get the speech-writing started. Mary told me she had been thinking of what I ought to say all day. She got started, and before I knew it, she handed it to me and searched for my approval as I read it aloud. I was totally impressed and agreed that it was the perfect speech for me. Mary and her friend got up to leave after a nice visit. Mary reminded me that she and Jon would pick me up at the office to go to Mobile.

"Don't forget to wear your black dress, chick," I reminded.

"Why black, Wynona?" they asked.

I grinned. "Tomorrow might as well be a funeral."

They both nodded their approval.

I took the three pages and began trying to memorize them. I read them over and over in front of the living room mirror. At eleven I gave it a rest and went to bed to get some sleep. I laid there starring at the ceiling. It was so quiet; I could hear the digital alarm clock breathing. Around three I gave up on sleep and turned on a movie to help me pass the time. Five o'clock. The movie ended, and I got in my wake-up shower and got dressed. I brewed up a pot of coffee. It was the best cup of coffee I had in years. I put on my black dress and headed to the office. It was seven fifteen.

It was overcast, cold, and raining. The weather man on TV said we would probably have severe storms most of the day. Eight-thirty. It was about an hour before Mary and Jon were due to show up. The phone rang, and I answered. It was Mathew, Gregory's probation officer.

"Just wanted you to know that sentencing has been moved back for five months," he said.

"You're kidding me, right? Why?" I asked.

"I have no idea. They didn't even tell me," he said.

"Okay. Thanks for calling," I said, dejected.

As I hung up the phone, the whole office shook and boomed. It was so dark outside that the rain hid the cars in the parking lot outside. I sat there. I don't know what time Mary called to let me know they were on their way. I explained about Mathew's call. I hung up and just watched the rain.

I don't know how much time passed; I decided I'd call Judge Kevin. When he answered, I told him about the extension on the sentencing. He said he would call a friend of his who worked as a federal probation officer to see what he could find out. About thirty minutes, Judge Kevin called me back.

"My buddy told me that it got postponed because no one contested the continuance," he said.

"I didn't know I had to. Can you give me the number for the federal attorney so I can call him and let him know I'd like to protest the extension?"

"Sure, Wynona. Let be find out what it is, and I'll give you a call right back."

Another thirty minutes passed, and he called with the number. His name was Michael. I dialed the number. His voice mail picked up immediately. Fuming, I blasted out a message I'm too ashamed to repeat. I sat down and composed a letter to the court explaining my objection to any further delay in the sentencing. In fact, I wanted it moved up to the earliest possible date. I sent a faxed copy of the letter to his office and mailed him the original. I was sitting quietly, boiling at my desk, when the phone rang. Mathew was on the other end.

"The federal attorney asked me to personally call you and let you know that there would be no more extensions." He was dead serious.

"Good," I said.

I hung up still simmering. As soon as the phone hit the desk, it started ringing again. *Who now?!* Well, Agent Bob was on the line and wasn't overjoyed at calling me.

"I just got off the phone with the federal prosecutor. He asked me to personally call you and let you know what's going on," he said.

He talked and talked but said absolutely nothing I wanted to hear.

I interrupted him and blurted out, "I have waited long enough. I just want to see Gregory in one of those orange jumpsuits that says 'Property of Baldwin County.' Are you guys following him still?"

"I'm sure we are, Wynona. Why?" he asked.

"Because he's gonna run. Y'all have given him way too much time. I'll bet he's already figured out how to get out the country. He's gonna get away!" I exclaimed.

"No, baby. I promise you he will be in court. Don't worry," he said, sounding patronizing.

I wasn't feeling consoled but just flat-out blown off. The only thing my phones calls had accomplished was to get a couple of calls to Gregory's handlers. It would still be five months until his sentencing.

The months dragged on again with nothing special happening. The day finally arrived for court. I woke up in a great mood and looked for my black dress. I was hoping for retribution and restitution. Kate had to work again. Mary and Jon picked me up for the ride over. My bookkeeper, Doris, decided she wanted to go, too. We headed to Mobile early so we could sit down and have lunch before court.

After we ate we walked the two city blocks to the federal courthouse. Court was on the second floor. When we got to the courtroom door, we noticed a sign on the right side that read "Do not enter while court is in session." So we looked through the glass window in the double doors. There was a man in an orange jumpsuit standing before the lady judge. I looked around and saw Agent Bob. He noticed us peeking through the glass. He got up and came out in the hallway to chat with me. He explained that we could go in the other door and take a seat in the back. We walked in, and, just like good Baptists, sat on the back pew.

I looked around the room as I took my seat. Court was about to start, but to my horror, Gregory was nowhere to be seen. Joshua, his parents, and sister were missing, too. I felt cold all the sudden. The judge sentenced the guy in front of her and called her next case. It was Gregory's.

Gregory's court appointed lawyer stood up and said, "Present, Your Honor."

Looking around, she motioned with her hands and asked, "Not you, counselor. Your client. Where is Gregory?"

"I don't know, Your Honor," he said, his head down.

"I don't care if you are here, counselor. Your client isn't. Let the record show the defendant has failed to appear before me as directed to do. I do hereby issue a bench warrant for his arrest. I would find my client if I were you, counselor," she said.

Her gavel split the air like thunder as it smashed on her bench. Court was adjourned. She thought she was mad. Whew! She didn't have any idea of what mad was.

I walked right up to the judge's bench. Agent Bob was standing there as the judge looked down at him from her seated position.

"How are you doing?" Agent Bob asked.

"You lied to me!" I yelled.

"How's that? I don't know what you're talking about!" he exclaimed.

"You promised me he would be here, that he was being watched. I told you he was gonna run, and you let him!"

I wanted to kick the skin off Agent Bob's shins. I stared coldly at him.

"You have two weeks to find that lowlife," I said.

"Oh Lord, then what?"

"Then I will find him for you. I will dot his eye, tie him up, and drop him off to you."

"Baby, you can't find him," he said.

"Oh yes, I can. There are ways."

"Baby, I am a federal agent. You can't be telling me this. If you do it, I will have to arrest you," he said.

"That'll be fine. I have done my research. It was a two hundred and fifty dollar fine and up to one hundred and eighty days in jail. I've put my money away, and I'm willing to do my time."

He just looked at me with shock in his eyes.

"Baby, I am a federal agent, and the federal judge is sitting right there listening to everything you say."

"Okay, dude, I thought we had already gotten this straight. You are a federal agent, she is a federal judge, and I am a redneck. You still have two weeks." I held my two fingers. I showed him both sides to make sure he counted them. "Two!" I walked away to get away from the stench.

"Let's head out, everyone. I can't stand to be around the crap anymore," I said as I approached my entourage. In a flash, we were gone.

The following Friday I was at work when the phone rang. I had just sat back down at my desk to eat lunch. It was an old boyfriend Edward. I had known him since elementary school. We dated on and off for five years. Currently we were off but still talked from time to time. There was excitement in his voice as he explained to me the events that had happened to him in the last three days.

"I was going to Pensacola to go shopping with my youngest daughter. We went through a roadblock where they were checking licenses and insurance. I don't know what made the officer pull me out of line but he did. He ran my license and told me they had a warrant for my arrest. The warrant was from a ticket that didn't get paid twelve years ago when I was married to my ex-wife. They handcuffed me and threw me in the back of a car and hauled me off to jail. While I was waiting to be transferred to BayMinette, where I would have to bond out from, they put me in general population in Pensacola. A guy sat down beside me. He didn't talk at first. I got bored then asked him what his name was. I thought he said Green. So I said, 'Green, what did you do?'

"'My name's not Green. It's Gregory,' he said.

"'So, Green, what did you do?' I asked again.

"Gregory smiled real big and told me, 'I've been on the run. I stole money from an insurance company in Gulf Shores. If I had stayed longer, I would have stole more. I did the crime, and I'm willing to do the time. When I get out, I'll never have to work another day in my life.'

"I asked him, 'Who did you steal it from?'

"'Wynona at Starfish. Do you know her?'

"I lied and said, 'No. Never heard of her. What did you do with the money, Green?'

"'I put four hundred thousand in Canada and the same amount here in the states. I have it in other people's names so it can't be traced back to me.'

"I asked him where he was running to, and he said, 'The courts took my passport so I couldn't leave the country. I found a guy who could help me get out. I paid him twenty five thousand dollars to let me catch a ride to Turkey on a freight ship. I just needed two more days for it to get here, and then I would have been home free. If some campers hadn't recognized my picture from the news, I would be halfway there by now.'"

Edward told me that when it was all over, to look him up. I suggested he not hold his breath. He didn't stay in the worst of it so who needed him anyway. I did thank him for telling me about Gregory, though. I found out from someone other than Agent Bob. What a surprise. I decided to call him and see if he would tell me more information.

I was so excited my hand was shaking when I dialed Agent Bob's number.

"Agent" was all he could get out before I interrupted him.

"Is it true?"

"Is what true, Wynona?"

"About Gregory getting caught," I said, busting with excitement.

"I was going to tell you in the morning, but yes, he's in custody."

"So he can't bond out again right?"

"That's right. He'll be right where he's at until sentencing next Friday at one."

"See you there Agent Bob."

"I don't doubt that for a minute, Wynona. See you then."

Next I called Mary to tell her what had happened. She just started laughing and said it could only happen to me. She and Jon will clear their calendars and pick me up. I went home to practice my speech for court. I practiced every night for two hours. I practiced so much I was beginning to lose my voice. I was ready, though. Finally, justice would be served.

The days that followed seemed like weeks as the hours dragged by. I tried to stay busy selling insurance so I would not think about it. It did not work. All I could do was think about how I was going to feel when I saw him. Friday came, and it was time to get ready to meet Mary and Jon. I woke up bright-eyed and bushy-tailed. I felt like I was walking on air as I walked to my closet once again to put on my black dress. I got dressed quickly and cruised straight to the office. I had just gone inside to pour myself a cup of coffee when Mary and Jon pulled up. Mary came inside. She said she was so excited she could not wait to go to Mobile. I looked at Mom and said I would call her after court. She told me she loved me as I was walking out the door. It seemed like the drive to Mobile took a week.

We arrived and parked across the street from the federal courthouse. I asked them where they wanted to go for lunch. Mary said she thought that cute little restaurant that we ate at before. We walked the short distance and took a seat. It was eleven o'clock. We sat and ate and went over the speech several times. The last time I read it, I teared up. Mary asked me if I would like for her to read it for me in court. I said yes. I was afraid I would be so mad when I saw him, I would start crying and not be able to speak. I handed her the speech. We were all anticipating what was about to happen.

We got to the courtroom and took our seat at the back. In the front of the courtroom, I could see the back of Gregory's head as he sat by his attorney. Court was about to start when Agent Bob and the federal attorney stood up and walked back to me. They asked me to step outside in the hallway. Mary and Jon followed us out.

"We wanted to let you know before he's sentenced that the most he would get would be forty one months. Gregory had something the big bosses thought would help on something else and gave him a deal."

"Dude, that's total crap. That pile of dung gets to take over a million dollars and try to murder me and that's all he's going to get?"

"It's the best that could be done." He tried to console me.

"We'll I guess it's better than him running free. But for the record, it is total crap. You tell that to your big bosses." I stormed back to the courtroom. This show had cost me millions, and I was intent on seeing the end. We all quietly took our seats. There was only Gregory and a man in an orange jumpsuit. As the clerk announced his name, the man in the orange jumpsuit stood up with the federal attorney. The judge cleared her throat and began to speak.

"Does the defendant have anything to say before I read the sentence?"

"I'm truly sorry for taking what I did. I just went crazy. My son died a little over a year ago, and I've been so depressed. I don't even know why I robbed those two banks."

"Sir, I'm really not in the mood to hear your excuses. You are to be confined for a term of four and one half years. You are guilty of the crime, and you will do all of this time. You are also ordered to pay immediate restitution totaling one hundred and forty thousand dollars. If you don't have the money all of your assets will be sold to cover the amount. Take him from my sight bailiff. Next case."

Gregory, his attorney, and the federal attorney all stood up and walked to where the judge was.

"Do you have anything to say to the court?" she asked.

"I'm sorry for what I did. I know nothing I can do can make it right."

The only thing that lowlife was sorry for was getting caught, I thought. His attorney addressed the judge.

"We have a deal, Your Honor."

I was suddenly furious with Agent Bob.

"The deal is off, Counselor."

"No, the deal is still good."

The judge began shaking her finger at him. "I'm wearing the black robe here! I said the deal's off. Your client voided that arrangement the day he skipped my court the last time. He's wasted enough of the court's time."

Gregory turned to his attorney and whispered.

"I said I was sorry. You said I wouldn't have—" the judge's gavel cracked through the air.

"You!"

Gregory spun his head around to face her.

"You have wasted more than enough of my time. If you say another word, I'll double your sentence right now and start adding to it for every second you are in my sight."

The judge's clerk leaned over and whispered something in her ear.

"By law all I can give you is forty-one months. Mark my words, you will spend every minute of it behind bars. After that you will serve forty-one months of supervised probation. If you screw up, you will serve those three years behind bars, too. So go ahead and test positive for drugs or alcohol. If I find out you have gotten so much as get a jay-walking ticket, I will add to it. Got me? Bailiff, remove this pariah from my sight."

A symphony played sweetly in my mind. Gregory was an alcoholic and abused Lortab, and probably other stuff, too. I stood there waiting for him to turn around so I could flip him off. The band in my mind stopped playing. *What about the money?* I realized that was the part of the deal that Agent Bob thought I might be upset about. How clever of him not to mention it.

He slowly walked out of the room with his head hanging low. He was in handcuffs and shackles. He still would not look at me. Once he left the room, I walked up to Agent Bob to hand him a letter that Mary had printed off the computer.

"You should save this for my file."

It was a letter from a friend of mine who is a Baptist preacher. He gets at least twenty-five thousand hits a day on his website. It stated that he prayed the courts would give Gregory life so that what he had done to me he could never do to anyone else. I turned to leave and turned around to look back. Agent Bob and the federal attorney were reading the letter. The judge spoke up and asked Agent Bob to bring it to her to read. I turned back around and started walking to my friends waiting for me at the door.

I was raising my hand to open the door when a little five-foot man got between me and the door. He asked me to stop. I asked him what I had done. He said I could not leave the courtroom until Gregory was safe in the van and it had left the parking lot. That lowlife still had more rights than me. Of course it could have had a little something to do with the last time I was in court. You know they really do not like it when you tell them you are going to dot someone's eye and drop him off to them. I guess it is an ego thing. Anyway, we took a seat. About ten minutes passed. The little dude got a call on his cell phone. He got off and told me now I could leave. I guess they were right to hold me there. If I had passed Gregory in the hall, I would have knocked him out. There went my last chance. At least his freedom had been taken away from him. I would have liked to have seen him get life, but something is better than nothing. I decided to ask Agent Bob about my money.

"I meant to ask you. What happens to my money?"

"If they do find it, they will give the IBM their money first. From there it's up to the judge to decide how it's distributed. I'm sorry it wasn't what you had hoped for."

So my money was gone, never to be seen again. He admitted he had stolen from me and the International

Baptist Mission Board. The IBM did not prosecute Gregory. If they had I never would have met him, and I would still have my purple house on the bluff, my money, and my life as I had always known it. It was time for a change. God had an intense way of getting my attention. I've decided to let him lead me down life's highway from now on.

AFTERWORD

Live life the best you can. Never steal or lie. Chances are if you see someone with money, it is because they set their goals and worked hard to achieve it. You can, too. Never give up. God has your back. I know he has mine. I am lucky, you know. You may not think so. Every day I wake up to check and see if I am still breathing, which I know sounds stupid, but I do. Every day is a gift from God. No matter what troubles come my way, I am going to have a good day.

My daddy always told me there was a silver lining in every cloud. After what Gregory had done to me, I thought Daddy was wrong. It ended up I was wrong, and Daddy was right. I could not pay my house note on the purple house so the bank finally decided to take it. They had every right.

I was sitting on the porch two days later after work. I was tired. I had been wondering how I was going to get my fortune back. A car pulled up. The real estate agent said he had some great news. The bank had agreed to pay me 1 percent of my loan to move in thirty days. I had a jumbo loan and thought that was great. I just thought they would kick me out for free. I agreed and told him I would make it happen. He left, and I started packing. I had years of stuff that I had collected and a lot of Little Dude's toys. I went uptown, which meant the first red light, and started looking behind stores for boxes. I did not have the money to buy anything. I collected some and started packing. It took me three weeks to move and store my furniture. I had no place to go but home to Mom. She took me in with open arms. She lived in the country. There was one bar, one fire station, and one small church. I thought I had died and gone to hell. There was nothing down there but the elderly.

I called the agent a week before I was supposed to move. I told him I would drop off the key and he could do his inspection. He was busy but his wife was at work and I could give it to her so I did. The next day my cell phone rang. It was him. He said he had never seen anything like it before. I said, "Look, dude, don't tell me it ain't clean. I cleaned on the purple house every day for three weeks."

"No, Wynona, it was too clean. I don't understand how that could be. Look, Wynona, most people that get foreclosed on take the appliances, door knobs—anything that is detachable. You took nothing and left us keys to two doors. I would like to know why," he said.

"That's how I was raised. My daddy told me if you don't keep your word then your word means nothing. If you don't have your word then you would be the poorest person I knew, even if you had millions. I said I would have it clean for you so I did. Now where's my check?"

He said the check was in the mail. *Good one*, I thought, but he was telling the truth. The check arrived a couple of days later. I rented a truck and lugged everything to Mom's house. I stuffed things into every nook and cranny to keep from having to pay for storage. I looked after Mom, who was sick, for months when I first moved in.

Ultimately, we found out she needed to have her gallbladder removed. She had come within hours of dying. A few days before we found all that out, I met David, my current husband. We tied the knot the day before Mother's Day. The Monday after, I got the following letter in the mail from my son. The funny thing is that the address on the envelope was totally wrong and should have never made it to me.

Dear Mom,

You are one of my heroes because you have influenced me all of my life. You have raised and taken care of me all of my life. Whenever I need something, you are always there for me. You never quit at anything you put your mind to. You are the best mom ever. Whenever I am with you, it is always a good thing. Without you I would not know what to do. I will always love you. You have always been the same through good times and bad. Hope you are happy all the time. You are number one.

Love,

David

I can only describe the way reading it made me feel as "touched by my angel."

There is a silver lining in every cloud. Sometimes it just takes you a while to find it.

When someone goes through something like I have, I'm told you are supposed to have learned something. Because the pain is so strong, even after all this time, it's hard to pen down just one thing. Before I let you in on my reflections, let me tell you something that happened the Christmas before Gregory got caught.

My younger sister, knowing I was broke and needing a place to vacation awhile with Little Dude, allowed me to stay at the penthouse we once owned together. I was trying to come up with some cash so I could put a few things under the Christmas tree. I took one of my last pieces of jewelry, a gold chain, to my friend's jewelry story. I paid about twenty five hundred dollars when I first bought it. I figured I'd be lucky if I just got a thousand for it. When he made the check out to me it read $3600.01. I was thrilled. I actually made money on the exchange. I gave my friend a huge hug and thanked him for making Little Dude's Christmas better.

We settled in for the week. Little Dude had a friend stay with us, and they were having a ball. One night I was lying in bed, reflecting on things and trying not to fall apart. Awhile passed, and I felt something wet land on my right cheek. I sat up in the bed and looked around. No one was in the room but me. I looked up to see if there was a water leak coming from the ceiling above. There was nothing. I wiped it from my face and lay back down. As I was trying to go to sleep, I felt a peace I had rarely felt in the past few years. I thought to myself that it must have been a tear from heaven. It was like God wanted me to know I wasn't alone, that he understood my pain, that he loved me.

So what have I learned then? Well, first, no one is totally alone in this world. You may not see God or things that remind you he's there, but he is. Second, I learned that I can forgive someone for doing evil, but evil things can't be forgiven. It's easier to trust in man than God. But with God, you don't have to worry about him breaking your trust. He is and always will be the beacon in the storm, so let him guide you home safely. I don't have money anymore, but I am as rich as any king. I'm rich in faith in God, and nobody can steal that from me.

God only gives you one life to live, but if you live it right, one's enough.

God bless. Peace out, dude.

Wynona

David
2003